"The most balanced team is one [...] strengths and skills. When introverts and extroverts stop competing for space and start filling the gaps, powerful things can happen. Mike masterfully pulls back the curtain on the struggles introverts face in the workplace and offers easy solutions that won't compromise who you are (or exhaust you in the process)."

**Jon Acuff**, *New York Times* bestselling
author of *Soundtracks*

"As an introvert, I learned the hard way that trying to be someone you're not leads to burnout, not success. I wish I'd had the wisdom, insights, and practical steps Mike Bechtle offers in this book years ago. This is a must-read for any introvert who wants to truly thrive in their work, not by changing who they are but by fully embracing their God-given strengths."

**Holley Gerth**, bestselling author of *The
Powerful Purpose of Introverts*

"In my work with professional speakers, I regularly mentor introverts who feel limited by their temperament. *The Introvert's Guide to Success in the Workplace* dissolves those myths, providing a logical, step-by-step process for introverts to achieve the same (or even greater) impact than their extroverted peers. Every introvert needs this resource in their library if they want to claim their spot as a top performer in any field!"

**Grant Baldwin**, author of *The Successful Speaker*
and founder and CEO of The Speaker Lab

"This book is one of a kind. Other books on this subject have convinced us that it's OK to be an introvert. This one makes it extremely practical, helping us to capitalize on the strengths of our temperament and translate them into success skills for work and life. It's not a how-to book on how to pretend to be an extrovert; it's a useful, helpful handbook on being our best selves so we can contribute powerfully and thrive authentically in the world we share with extroverts."

**Ken Gonyer**, former CEO of Choice Books

"Whoever said 'the loudest person wins' was just plain wrong. From his own personal and professional experience, author Mike Bechtle demonstrates that being introverted is not a handicap. It's not even a weakness. In fact, it's a strength working in our favor when understood and used properly. In his engaging writing style, Bechtle combines scholarship, story, and practical and proven action steps to help introverted readers engage the ever-present creative tension between acceptance and adjustment—accepting our personality in a healthy way while also making adjustments that are both meaningful and manageable to become the best version of ourselves. With a focus on the workplace, the principles in this outstanding book apply to solopreneurs, business owners, executives, managers, team leaders, and employees. In other words, if you're an introvert with a job, you need to read this book!"

**Ramon Presson**, PhD, licensed counselor and author of *When Will My Life Not Suck?*

# THE INTROVERT'S GUIDE TO SUCCESS IN THE WORKPLACE

# THE INTROVERT'S GUIDE TO SUCCESS IN THE WORKPLACE

Becoming Confident
in a Culture of
Extroverted Expectations

## DR. MIKE BECHTLE

Revell
a division of Baker Publishing Group
Grand Rapids, Michigan

Published by Revell
a division of Baker Publishing Group
Grand Rapids, Michigan
www.revellbooks.com

Printed in the United States of America

Library of Congress Cataloging-in-Publication Data
Names: Bechtle, Mike, 1952– author.
Title: The introvert's guide to success in the workplace : becoming confident in a culture of extroverted expectations / Dr. Mike Bechtle.
Description: Grand Rapids, Michigan : Revell, a division of Baker Publishing Group, 2023. | Includes bibliographical references.
Identifiers: LCCN 2023009835 | ISBN 9780800742775 (paperback) | ISBN 9780800745028 (casebound) | ISBN 9781493443437 (ebook)
Subjects: LCSH: Interpersonal communication. | Confidence. | Success in business.
Classification: LCC BF637.C45 B4295 2023 | DDC 153.6—dc23/eng/20230415
LC record available at https://lccn.loc.gov/2023009835

Scripture quotations are from *THE MESSAGE*, copyright © 1993, 2002, 2018 by Eugene H. Peterson. Used by permission of NavPress. All rights reserved. Represented by Tyndale House Publishers, Inc.

The names and details of the people and situations described in this book have been changed or presented in composite form in order to ensure the privacy of those with whom the author has worked.

Baker Publishing Group publications use paper produced from sustainable forestry practices and post-consumer waste whenever possible.

23   24   25   26   27   28   29         7   6   5   4   3   2   1

To Jacob.
God created you
because it made him happy.
Then he gave you to us
and it made us happy.
You bring joy to everyone around you . . .
and we're so grateful for you!

# CONTENTS

# INTRODUCTION

It's five in the morning, and I've arrived at a Starbucks near my house. I come here often because it's a great place to write without distraction. It's a drive-thru location, so most of the other customers will stay outside in their cars, and I'll have the inside practically to myself.

I like that. For me, early mornings are a time to enjoy the quiet. It's when I build up my energy for the day. It was dark as I drove here, and there's not much traffic yet.

I exchange a few words with the cashier as she takes my order. She smiles as she talks—it's a brief, warm, human connection. Behind the counter it is busy and noisy even at this early hour. The baristas are moving at 1.25 speed to provide customers with their caffeinated jolts for the day. Utensils are clacking, steam is hissing, and the chatter is constant.

I take my coffee back to my usual table by the window where I can watch the world wake up. It's much quieter in the sitting area. I watch the sun yawning its way over the horizon, and I savor a world that's not in a hurry. I know the day will be filled with meetings and conversations and productivity and challenges, but I can handle that well if I start my day slowly. It feels like I've stopped at an emotional gas station and topped off my tank to prepare for the day.

Before long they turn the music on (rap at the moment), disturbing the quiet and threatening my solitude. I came prepared for the music, and as I do each day, I pull out my secret weapon to help me retreat into focused silence: *my noise-canceling headphones.*

I always figured these were invented by an introvert who worked best in a quiet environment, but it turns out they were created by a sound engineer on an international flight back in 1978. The flight attendants gave passengers simple headphones to listen to music, but the cabin noise was loud enough to block most of the tunes. So this engineer used his drink napkin to scribble out his ideas on how to eliminate background noise, which led to the noise-canceling technology we use today. His name was Dr. Amar Bose. He couldn't make the airplane quieter, so he found a way to keep the noise out and focus on what he wanted to hear.[1]

Or think about scuba gear. If we want to see things deep in the ocean, we can't survive without it. Sure, it would just be easier if we could become fish—but that's not going to happen. That's what being an introvert working in a world of extrovert expectations can feel like. People assume we should just become extroverts and fit in, but that's as realistic as growing fins and gills. Instead, we accept the reality of the situation and find creative ways to function in that foreign environment.

We're not fish, and we're not extroverts.

We're *introverts*—and we have everything we need to negotiate the world of work with stellar results. Our job is to step up and become the best version of ourselves, and in this book, you'll learn how!

## Where It All Started

"Nothing will ever become of your son," I heard my kindergarten teacher tell my parents. "He's too shy."

I don't have a lot of early memories of school, but that one stuck. I was a little surprised that she said it while I was standing there, as if I was too young to notice. I'm sure the conversation continued, but I don't remember hearing it. All I recall is my five-year-old's interpretation of what I heard:

- If you're going to succeed in life, you can't be shy.
- I wasn't sure what "shy" meant, but it didn't sound good. It implied that there was something wrong with me that needed to be fixed.
- It couldn't be fixed. It sounded permanent.
- It sounded like a defect that would make my entire life "less than."

Over time, those early words became my identity. I didn't know any better, so I wasn't really suffering; I just figured I wasn't in the same league as other kids. They were the "winners"—outgoing and friendly and warm, hanging out with others who were the same. I would hang out with the "losers"—the quieter kids and the misfits. It wasn't because I was drawn to them but because that's where I felt I belonged.

After all, a professional (my teacher) had declared my position, so it must be accurate.

Since I believed that about myself, I assumed everyone else believed it too. *He's the shy kid,* I figured they must be thinking. *I wouldn't want to be his friend.* That's a heavy burden for a kid to carry. But I didn't know there were any alternatives.

One day, in my fifth-grade physical education class, we divided up into two teams to play kickball. The captains took turns selecting who they wanted on their team, and soon I was the only one left. The good news is that the captains fought over me. The bad news is that they were fighting to *get rid of* me. "You take him," one captain said. "No, that's OK," said the other, "You can just keep him."

It was uncomfortable but not unexpected. It simply reinforced what I assumed was true: I was at the bottom of the pecking order among my peers. It was my perception, so it became my reality. I convinced myself that I was just a quiet person; things would always be this way, and there was nothing I could do about it. It also meant I would never be successful because I couldn't be noisier. I saw all the outgoing kids in my school—their success in friendships, in opportunities, and in life—and knew that couldn't be me.

I was stuck, and it didn't seem fair. I wanted to change, but I knew that I couldn't and I had proof: the words of my teacher.

## It's Not Just a Kid Problem

Once I hit high school, I learned some coping skills to survive. I was still quiet on the inside, but I figured out how to make a few good friends and connect with them. Outside of that group, I still felt out of place. The popular kids seemed to be the outgoing ones, but I was more reflective. When I found myself in conversations with them, I always struggled to think of quick responses. They would say something, and I had to pause to put my words in order. That hesitation always felt like uncertainty, which reinforced my view of myself.

I remember a guy on the football team asking me a question. It took me a few seconds to put my response together—long enough for him to say, "Why can't you just say what you're thinking? Spit it out!" That paralyzed my thoughts even more, and I can still see him walking away, shaking his head. About thirty seconds later I had formed a perfect, clever response—but he was gone.

Extroverts tend to think faster and shape their thoughts by talking about them. Introverts like me tend to think deeper and shape our words by thinking about them first. In that conversation, I wasn't done thinking. He hadn't started thinking.

## Nobody's Stuck

Our earliest life experiences form the foundation of our self-image. If introverts are compared to extroverts often enough, they'll see themselves as inferior and in need of change. If they're celebrated, they'll gain a healthy view of their introversion from the start.

Fortunately, a sense of inferiority can be overcome with a healthy exposure to truth at any age. That's what we'll be tackling throughout this book. We'll be challenging inaccurate paradigms and replacing them with true ones. If you still feel like you need to become more extroverted, you're on a certain path toward frustration and failure. Discovering and embracing your introversion is the superhighway to finding your identity and purpose.

You're about to become free.

## Thank God I'm an Introvert

I love being an introvert. Seriously. I wouldn't want it any other way.

That hasn't always been true. Growing up as an introvert in a world that seemed filled with extroverts wasn't easy, and I wished I could be as confident and outgoing and personable as everyone else appeared to be. I felt out of place, like a sloth living in the monkey exhibit at the zoo.

As we grow up, we see a world where successful people speak easily and know exactly what to say. On television we see talk show hosts, politicians, and celebrities who are fluent communicators. We may notice salespeople, leaders, lawyers, and even hairdressers make conversation easily for hours at a time. Since extroverts are good at talking, they're the ones we hear from the most. That's why it *feels* like it's an extrovert's world.

*But it's not.*

While it may feel like everyone else is extroverted, that's not true. Research shows that up to 50 percent of the population consists of introverts.[2] That means there are about the same number of us introverts as extroverts, so we're not in the minority. We're just not as obvious because we think more than we talk (we're fluent in "silence"). When extroverts are doing most of the talking, it seems like they're in the majority, which can make us feel at a disadvantage. Based on what we see on the surface, we might conclude we don't have what it takes to succeed because we have the wrong temperament.

This book challenges that perception. We have exactly the temperament we need to navigate life successfully and make an amazing impact in the world. We don't need to compete against extroverts; we just need to step up and take our place as coresidents of the planet!

A lot of introverts don't understand that perspective yet, thinking we're "not enough" because we're not as outgoing as other people. That's a damaging perception; it's untrue, and it's time for it to change.

It's time for a whole new paradigm—one that recognizes the unique contribution and value that only introverts can bring to the world. If we try to become like extroverts, we rob everyone of the things only we can offer.

It's time to move from *comparison* to *contribution*.

Let's discover what that contribution looks like—and how we can make it happen.

# Where the Journey Began

If we held an introvert conference, what would it look like?

Unknown

The scene is still fresh in my mind because the feelings were strong. The work team I was on had come together to meet our new boss and catch her vision for the future. There were about a dozen of us sitting around a long rectangular table, and I was in the front corner—right next to our leader. She stood and asked questions, captured ideas on a flip chart, and explored ideas from the group. It was a fascinating discussion, and she had an engaging style that showed she cared about the experience of the group.

I was listening carefully and scribbling copious notes about the ideas being shared. I felt positive about the direction we were heading, and even the fast-paced, noisy energy of the group. It was encouraging, and I knew I'd be processing the discussion for hours if not days after we were done.

Near the end of our time, our new leader turned to me and said, "Mike, you've been really quiet. What are you thinking?"

I went blank and felt a quick wave of terror. I had been fully engaged in the meeting, but I had been listening instead of talking. I was taking everything in so I could think through it and form my opinions later after processing them. But in the moment, I was caught completely off guard. The room got quiet, and everyone was staring, waiting for my response. I wanted to say something intelligent and impress my new boss, but my tank of cleverness was empty.

The silence probably lasted only a second or two before I mumbled something sort of relevant but not impactful. She definitely didn't write it on the flip chart. That second or two seemed like an eternity. When I left the meeting I wasn't thinking about the energizing ideas I'd heard or the potential for our team. I was beating myself up for a poor performance, making assumptions about what my new boss must think of me.

After years in the corporate environment, I've worked with many others who had similar experiences in all sorts of environments. Introverted construction workers complain that others seem comfortable interacting during morning meetings on the job site, but it takes a lot more energy for them to participate. Retail salespeople are expected to spend their day making phone calls in an open floor plan where everyone works together, but they find it draining and want to escape to an empty conference room where no one can listen in. When coworkers in a small business go out together after work, the introverted ones just want to go home, especially if the group is going someplace crowded and noisy.

"What's wrong with me?" I hear from many of these introverts. "Why can't I be more outgoing and social?" They don't dislike people—in fact, they usually enjoy the people they work with. They just seem to run out of steam right when the extroverts are ramping up. Introverts often find themselves pretending to be outgoing and to enjoy the energy of interaction, but that can be even more draining.

I remember feeling that way, and it seemed I had only two options:

I could try to change who I was.
I could give up and accept my limitations.

Neither of those struck me as positive. Changing my temperament sounded like a lot of work. Giving up sounded like, well . . . giving up. I needed a different solution, one where I could be myself but thrive in any environment.

That's where my journey began—and it's where you and I are headed.

## Making Sense in the Darkness

Somewhere along the line, I heard the term *introvert*. It was a fairly new term to me since nobody was talking much about it at that time. I looked up the definition: "A person who prefers calm environments, limits social engagement, or embraces a greater than average preference for solitude. . . characterized by concern primarily with their own thoughts and feelings."[1]

For the first time, I saw words that described how I felt that didn't seem negative. It didn't feel like the bad thing I had been trying to overcome but a normal thing for the way I was wired.

It turned out that researchers have been studying introversion for over a hundred years. But most of that time, there was an underlying assumption: extroversion was positive and desirable, and introversion was negative and undesirable. For example, most studies used a measuring scale where extroverted behavior was at the top of the scale (desirable) and introverted behavior was at the bottom (undesirable). So, the "ideal" was at one end, and the other end was the "opposite of ideal."

This would be like saying, "beach vacations (score of 100) are better than mountain vacations (score of 0)." The person making that scale was probably sitting on the sand with a bunch of noisy friends and saying, "It just doesn't get any better than this." Then someone else says, "I wonder what a mountain vacation would be like?" The group responds, "BORING! Why would anybody want to vacation in the mountains?" The underlying assumption is that everyone knows that a beach vacation is great, so everything else is measured against that standard. Since a trip to the mountains would be a "non-beach" vacation, it must be at the opposite end of the fun scale.

That type of introvert measurement was still happening in the late 1980s, around the same time Dr. Stephen Covey described how society switched from valuing *character* to *personality* as the criteria for success.[2] Previously, people respected a person based on how much they were characterized by integrity, humility, courage, patience, industry, and so on—not on how gregarious or outgoing they were. But when people learned they could get better results by displaying the characteristics of an extrovert, it became the new standard. Want success in life, friendships, and business? Pretend to be more outgoing and friendly, and position yourself to make others like you.

Introversion wasn't something to be applauded and valued. With personality as the primary measurement, introverts were considered "not extroverts"—which meant that introversion was something to be fixed.

## The Shift

In 2003, Jonathan Rauch wrote an article in the *Atlantic* called "Caring for Your Introvert" that went viral (in a mostly nondigital world). "Introverts may be common," he said. "But they are also among the most misunderstood and aggrieved groups in America, possibly the world."[3] I felt the empathy immediately, as if someone was finally giving a voice to my inner conundrum. It was like a glass of ice water in the heat of the Arizona desert where I'd grown up.

Around the same time, Marti Olsen Laney published *The Introvert Advantage*, one of the first books to build a comprehensive case for the value of introverts. Then Susan Cain presented a TED Talk called "The Power of Introverts," which still ranks among the most-viewed TED Talks of all time more than ten years later. She followed it in 2012 with her bestselling book *Quiet: The Power of Introverts in a World That Can't Stop Talking*, which touched a chord in the lives of millions of introverts who suddenly felt noticed and validated. In 2020, Holly Gerth wrote *The Powerful Purpose of Introverts*, and people who had struggled their entire lives with feeling "less than" began to see that they had something of great value to offer the world and didn't have to be at the mercy of those expecting them to be something they weren't.

The floodgates were opened, and more and more resources have been developed that carry this message for introverts: *You're OK just the way you are—and you're designed to make a difference*. People have found freedom from years of being compared to extroverts. We aren't just worth accepting; we're worth celebrating for the unique contribution we make in society.

There's still a long way to go, but the foundation has been built. That's step one. Not every introvert has realized their personal value, but the resources to help them get there are finally available. We've built a case for the remarkable value of introversion.

"That's great," the introvert says. "I see that I have something to contribute. I feel a lot better now—*but I still have to work in a world of extroverts*. I need practical skills for daily taking my place alongside other temperaments and navigating that world with precision. I need help working with people who might measure my performance by the outgoing, high-energy standards of extroverts. How can I be completely myself and contribute on an equal footing with extroverts in a business setting?"

That's step two, and it's the focus of this book.

I found success in the business world when I figured out that (a) I was an introvert, (b) I could never become an extrovert, and (c) pretending to be one was the quickest path to failure and discouragement. I learned to celebrate the way I was wired, discover my unique strengths, and then capitalize on them. That freed me to do what needed to be done in ways that extroverts could never come close to doing as well. I learned how to relate and interact on my own terms instead of their terms, win their respect, and make a difference. I found that it was possible for extroverts to value me for everything I had to offer.

An introvert isn't second-best, like the "first runner-up" in a beauty pageant. An introvert is actually "the best"—and so is an extrovert—because we're both operating in our uniqueness. Introverts can make an impact at work that extroverts can't even imagine doing (and vice versa).

## Catch the Vision

How will we get there? Here's an overview of the journey.

We won't spend a lot of time on step one, since there are so many great resources available. But we'll review the basics to make sure we're starting with a solid foundation. For some, this will be new information about their personal value. For others, it will be a chance to fine-tune what they've already discovered. Either way, we'll make sure we're crystal clear on the unique value of introverts.

Then we'll move to step two, where we'll learn a series of Master Moves that enable us to use our introversion as our superpower in our work environment. When we're done, here's what you can expect:

- You'll have the confidence to be completely yourself, without intimidation.
- You'll gain the respect of the extroverts you work with—colleagues, bosses, customers, vendors, and employees.
- You'll know how to manage your energy for peak performance.
- You won't feel the need to pretend you're more outgoing than you are.
- You'll be able to contribute in meetings and build respect in ways that are natural to you.
- You'll be able to speak in front of groups with confidence by being yourself.
- Your self-talk will build you up instead of tear you down.
- You'll be able to use your unique strengths to lead others effectively.
- You'll know how to become visible at work.
- You'll excel in whatever role you choose, even those usually associated with extroverts.
- You'll love going to work each day because you're working in your sweet spot.
- You'll excel in teamwork.
- You'll become bilingual because you have ESL fluency (Extrovert as a Second Language).
- You'll be an expert in the powers of influence, relationship building, leading, building trust, and compassion.
- You'll capitalize on your natural sensitivity to what's happening with others and in your environment.
- You'll know how to network in a unique way that goes beyond what extroverts can do.

You get to break unhealthy patterns and become the best version of yourself. It means growing and changing and gaining new skills that fit who you are, not someone else.

Is it easier to talk to others if you're an extrovert? Usually—but that doesn't mean you can't become a highly effective communicator. Talking is only one of the many differences between introverts and extroverts, so it's not the only thing to focus on—or even the main thing. This book will build your confidence in using your words with impact. And remember, success comes from drawing on every strength you have, not just your words.

I'll be your tour guide for this journey. I won't be teaching you a one-size-fits-all approach that guarantees results. Instead I'll walk with you on the journey as a fellow introvert, helping you craft your own personalized process that will work for you. This is *your* journey, not mine.

I'm just the guy with some insider information and experience.

My goal for this book isn't to help you just survive; it's to help you thrive in ways you can't imagine. I want to help you catch a new vision, move into that vision, and change the world.

I want you to be so impactful that extroverts say, "I wish I could be like them!"

# PART 1

# INTROVERTS AT WORK

In the game charades, you stand in front of a group and act out a phrase or idea, trying to get everyone to guess what it is—without using words. If you're an introvert, charades probably isn't your favorite party game.

- You have to stand in front of a group.
- You have to act something out with motions, body movements, and expressions.
- If the group guesses correctly, you feel better—but the whole process is way out of your comfort zone.
- If the group doesn't guess correctly, nobody says anything—but you feel like you let your team down and they're silently judging you.
- It can make you feel like others are better than you and you don't measure up.
- Everyone else looks like they're having a great time, and you feel like you're the only one who's hating the experience. But you smile and laugh anyway so no one notices.

I've often thought that if I had a choice between playing charades and having bamboo shoots jammed under my fingernails, I'd choose the latter. I've also thought that to survive in an extrovert world, I had to keep smiling and laughing as I played, pretending I was OK.

What if you had to play charades all day, every day for your entire life? That's what life can feel like for introverts who still have a "less than" mindset—playacting so we can make it through each day, pretending to be somebody we aren't. It can feel like there's no alternative, and it's exhausting.

There's another way. It's not about cosmetic work; it's about inside work. But it's not about willpower, which runs out over time. *The key to genuine change in our lives is to change the way we think.*

Thriving in a work environment comes from two things:

1. Fully accepting and celebrating our natural temperament.
2. Capitalizing on the unique strengths of that temperament to craft a contribution no one else can make.

Many of us believe we have to become something we're not in order to succeed—which is about as realistic as a watermelon changing into a sailboat. Real success can happen when we change our perspective and put all our energy into becoming the best possible version of who we already are.

This doesn't mean we ignore learning new skills that can help us thrive simply because they feel uncomfortable. It means accepting who we are, then adding and perfecting the skills needed in an extroverted workplace to make a serious impact. It's unhealthy to use our introversion as an excuse for not moving forward. We want to be fully alive, so we go through the process of learning and growing.

That's what this section is about—how we *think* (which is the foundation for everything else). We'll learn the skills we need later, but we'll start by looking at four things:

- *The introvert revival*—how people have traditionally viewed introverts, and how that has changed over the past couple of decades. Society is learning to value the contributions of introverts, but there are still longstanding expectations of how we need to perform in the workplace.
- *Mind games*—how we view others and the unconscious biases that skew our perception of them. We often believe we know exactly what extroverts are thinking. In most cases, we're mistaken and often totally wrong.
- *Myth busters*—what people commonly get wrong about us and the truths they overlook. Even introverts might believe these misconceptions, so we need to recognize and challenge them.
- *How to talk to yourself*—the danger in talking to ourselves incorrectly and not getting input from others. To see ourselves accurately, we need to avoid becoming too introspective or focusing on our inner dialogue. Self-examination can become toxic when it's not clarified by the feedback and perspective of others.

Building an accurate, enabling mindset means replacing what Zig Ziglar called "stinking thinking" with a new way of seeing ourselves and others with accuracy. (Research shows that we have about fifty thousand thoughts per day, and 70–80 percent of them are negative.[1])

Even if you're a complete introvert, you can excel in a business setting. We'll talk about those skills (superpowers, even) that precisely fit who you are. Then you can add new skills for thriving in the workplace. As you practice new skills and they improve over time, your confidence will grow and you'll make the biggest possible impact.

If our mindset is wrong, any new skills we learn will simply become coping mechanisms. We'll be operating from weakness, not strength. Our thoughts determine our beliefs, which determine our feelings, which determine our actions.

Let's build a strong foundation in our mindset so we become ready to work on the mechanics of change.

2

# The Introvert Revival

I may be quiet, but I have worlds inside.

Unknown

There's a huge upscale apartment complex right in the middle of downtown Los Angeles that takes up two or three city blocks. I've driven past it many times over the years. The buildings are hard to miss, because they're right up against the freeway I take to get home if I've been working at a local company that day. Since it's usually afternoon rush hour and the traffic is stopped, I have plenty of time to notice. I'm typically facing at least a two-hour drive. Thousands of drivers experience the same thing each day, and the long, exhausting commute is on everyone's mind.

One day a massive banner appeared on the side of the building that read, "If you lived here, you'd be home by now." My first thought was, *What great marketing. That message is obviously designed to hit the pain point of every driver on this road.* I wondered how many people moved there because of that sign.

My second thought came from deep inside my introvert self: *Who in their right mind would want to live right in the middle of downtown?* I've been in that area in the evening occasionally, and the streets were filled with almost as many people as there were during the day. It reminded me of occasional trips I've made to New York City, walking through Times Square or Manhattan late at night. The first time I heard the expression "The City That Never Sleeps," I thought, *Is that supposed to be a good thing?*

A few weeks later, I was back in downtown Los Angeles connecting with seminar participants before beginning a session. Lawrence was the first to arrive, and we were just getting acquainted. In that area, traffic is usually on everyone's mind, so it's a great place to begin a conversation. I asked, "So, how long did it take you to commute this morning?" He responded, "About five minutes."

"That's it?" I asked. "Where do you live?"

"In those big apartments down the block," he responded. "I walked here this morning."

I knew this would be one conversation I couldn't pass up. "So, what made you move there? And how do you like it?"

"I've been there about seven months, and I love it. I can't imagine living anywhere else. For one thing, I sold my car and either walk or rideshare everyplace. If I go on a trip, I just rent a car." I kept listening and Lawrence kept talking: "But the biggest thing is the energy of living in the city. At the end of an exhausting workday, there's nothing better than having things to do, people to meet, places to explore. Every night is a new adventure. I can't imagine going home to an empty house; it would be too quiet."

Lawrence was an extrovert and felt like he was living in nirvana. I'm an introvert, and I felt like he had just described life at the rim of an active volcano, complete with fire and brimstone.

## Pain Points

If you're like me, you may have envied how comfortable extroverts seem in conversation. At work, they don't hesitate to say what they're thinking. People call them the "movers and shakers," and it's easy to believe that if you want to succeed, you need to become an extrovert. Or at least pretend to be an extrovert.

Years ago, a college professor named William Pannapaker used one of his classes as a case study, having them complete a temperament survey that was popular at the time. Even though he had the normal mix of outgoing, engaged students and less vocal, less engaged students, they all answered the questions in a way that tagged them as extroverts. He knew this wasn't accurate, so he dug deeper.

It turned out that every student assumed extroversion was positive and introversion was negative. So, when asked, "Would you rather go to a party or stay home and read a book?" they saw partygoing as positive and reading as negative. The introverts knew the other students would see their responses, and they didn't want to be seen in a negative light—so they chose the most socially acceptable response.

Pannapaker writes, "Given that introversion is frowned upon almost everywhere in US culture, the test might as well have said, 'Would you prefer to be cool, popular and successful—or weird, isolated and a failure?' When debriefing the exercise in a class discussion, students generally assumed that "introversion was a kind of mental illness."[1]

That study reflected the perspective of society in general. Both extroverts and introverts failed to appreciate the unique temperament of an introvert. After all, if introversion was seen as a bad thing, why would anyone want to explore it?

Fortunately, someone did.

## The Introvert Awakening

Researchers in the mid-twentieth century knew that more work on the subject needed to be done, so they began to explore the possibility that introversion wasn't bad, just different. They also discovered that while Americans placed a higher value on extroversion, some other cultures (such as Asian countries) placed a higher value on quiet contemplation. Since up to 50 percent of the US population could be classified as introverted, researchers took notice. They went on a quest to get a more accurate picture of what introversion was all about.

People knew the characteristics of extroverts but didn't know much about introverts. Originally, introverts were simply described with a single perception by most people: *Thinks often about himself/herself.*[2] But since everyone is a unique combination of traits, we can't just classify ourselves as "quiet" and extroverts as "noisy." That stereotype doesn't do us any good.

The difference is where a person draws *energy*. Extroverts get their energy from focusing outwardly, favoring action over deep thinking. At the same time, they get drained when they spend too much time alone.

Introverts focus inwardly and need time alone to recharge. We can function well in groups, but it drains our energy. We prefer fewer relationships, but deeper ones.

Does that sound like you? Everyone is unique, but consider these general characteristics of each group.

### Extroverts

- They consider the world of other people and things to be "home." (After a full day at a conference, they look for others who want to meet up for a while.)
- They don't bottle up their emotions because they let them out little by little in conversation. (They form

their ideas by talking about them, and their emotions are attached to their thoughts.)

- They can be easily distracted. (They'll talk about several ideas as each comes up, even before they finish the previous one.)
- They have a bias for action. (They would rather just grab a wrench and take the plumbing apart than first study how to do it.)
- They're sociable. (At a social event, they want to connect with as many people as possible.)
- They get their energy from outside of themselves— from connecting with other people. (If they're low on energy, they'll grab their phone to arrange to meet a couple of friends.)
- They make decisions quickly. (They don't stress over ensuring they're making the right decision. They just decide, then tweak it if it doesn't work.)
- They're the same in public and private. (They're "just who they are" no matter what situation they're in.)

### Introverts

- We can't focus well if it's too noisy. (We turn down the car stereo when we're looking for an address.)
- We take longer to make decisions because we need to process the options first. (We're the last one to order at a restaurant if the menu has too many choices.)
- We often prefer writing over speaking. (If someone calls us, we'll let it go to voicemail so we have time to think of how to respond—then we'll text our reply.)
- We come up with solutions through creative thinking. (We don't just look at the facts; we consider the ramifications of each decision and how it will impact others.)

- We're reflective and consider our "inner world" to be our home. (We usually come up with great responses, but not until the conversation has ended.)
- We look forward to being alone. (If someone cancels dinner plans at the last minute, we see it as a gift—even if we really like that person.)
- We're exhausted after being in a large group setting for very long. (We'll make several trips to the restroom whether we need to or not, just to have a couple of minutes to give ourselves a shot of energy.)
- We retreat into our own minds to rest when we feel drained. (While sitting alone in a quiet setting and doing nothing, we can feel our energy coming back.)
- We learn best by working alone rather than in a group. (We don't know what we think during a discussion; that happens when we can process alone later.)
- We have fewer friends, but closer ones. (We prefer quality over quantity in relationships.)
- We have a "public self" and a "private self." (The private self is our real world where we live, from which we step into the world of others with our public self.)

Finally, we are finding our voices as introverts in the workplace—without needing to become extroverts. People have started talking about the value of introverts, recognizing the unique contribution we make in the world. If we Google "the value of introverts," we'll find a treasure trove of information for overcoming feelings of inferiority. The literature proves introverts are significant, and there are a ton of resources available to reinforce our personal worth.

In other words, we "have a place," and have been proven to be an untapped resource in many situations.

But we still live in an extrovert-biased world. Most people haven't seen all the research and still believe it's probably better to be an extrovert. Extroverts likely know the least about all this research, because they haven't read any of it. Why would they, if their own experience seems to be so much easier and impactful (and more fun) than an introvert's approach?

I think it's interesting that there is so much respect and admiration for introverts who have had a huge impact on society, such as Abraham Lincoln, Mahatma Gandhi, Albert Einstein, Warren Buffet, Rosa Parks, Dr. Seuss, Steven Spielberg, JK Rowling, Steve Jobs, and Bill Gates. No one questions the huge difference they have made in our world. But we didn't know they were introverts—we just liked what they did. We think, *They were effective. They made a difference. They started a movement.* But we never stop and think, *Oh, and by the way, they were introverts.*

Society praises the impact but ignores the process. This is why Susan Cain writes, "There's zero correlation between being the best talker and having the best ideas."[3]

It's still an uphill battle. Marti Olsen Laney writes, "The introvert is pressured daily, almost from the moment of awakening, to respond and conform to the outer world."[4] Even if we read the literature and learn to appreciate our unique temperament, *we still have to go to work*—and "it's a jungle out there." It's one thing to feel good; it's another thing to navigate the extrovert-infested waters of today's workplace.

Fortunately, it's no longer about trying to compete in that world. It's about learning how to come alongside extroverts as equal but different contributors. We don't need to survive; we need to flourish.

## Making It Work at Work

We spend forty-plus hours per week (if we're in an office setting) with bosses and coworkers who might not understand the unique value of introverts. They often have expectations shaped by the extrovert perspective they've experienced. In a hybrid or remote setting where we're working from home some or all of the time, we still have the same communication challenges—plus we're expected to be on video when we do connect.

In the office, it's tough enough to become "seen" by others to be able to get ahead; in a remote work setting, or out on a jobsite working independently, it's even tougher because we're even less visible. How do we succeed and make an impact without pretending to be somebody we're not?

One example would be teaching in a university setting—a career that often attracts introverts who think there won't be as many social demands, and they'll be able to research and study in the confines of their office. What they often overlook is that while there are long periods of working alone, there are brief (but frequent) periods of intense social interaction. They have to teach classes, interview for various positions, attend and present at conferences, and participate in regular meetings. They're expected to contribute by jumping into discussions to call attention to themselves.

In most such situations, there's not a lot of mentoring to help an introvert navigate those treacherous waters. When I took a job as an associate professor at a university, the interview process consisted of fifteen events in just over two days. I had a series of high-stakes interviews with prospective colleagues, department heads, grad students—all the way up to the president of the university. I had to teach classes with about ten faculty members sitting in the back row taking notes on their clipboards, and I had to deliver a public lecture for anyone to attend. Each meal was shared with multiple people for the chance to have a "relaxed" networking opportunity. Each event was in an unfamiliar setting, and everything was scheduled back-to-back to save time—which meant I had no downtime to recharge.

The entire process was geared toward (and probably designed by) extroverts, and I was being evaluated through that lens. The challenge was to let my introvert strengths shine in that setting and resist the temptation to pretend I was an extrovert. It worked, and I got the job.

I had trouble forming coherent thoughts for a week afterward.

During the hiring process, it's natural for an interviewer to be impressed by an applicant's charisma and demeanor. *I like this person*, they think. *They would be a good fit here.* While chemistry is valuable, it's not the only thing. Too often, they end up hiring a likable (extroverted) person who does a mediocre job while overlooking a deep-thinking introvert capable of bringing a thoughtful, strategic approach to any position.

## How Introverts Thrive at Work

So, how does an introvert overcome those common expectations and thrive in the workplace? By becoming 100 percent yourself—a world-class introvert living and working through the filter of your unique temperament. As comedian Steve Martin said, "Be so good they can't ignore you."[5]

That doesn't mean taking an "Eeyore approach" to life, feeling like you're just stuck being a backup player on the introvert bench. Succeeding means fully accepting your temperament, then being intentional about growing and changing and capturing new skills that completely match who you are.

If you're a cheetah, you'll never become an eagle. True success comes when you get a running coach, not a flying coach.

# 3

# Mind Games

Every time a cashier asks if I found everything OK, I lie and say "yes" just so there won't be any more questions.

Unknown

You'll have the provost of the local university in your seminar today," my colleague told me. I had flown to this college town the day before to teach a public seminar at a local hotel, and my friend was the sales partner responsible for filling the class. I always try to connect with as many people as possible before the session begins, so he was filling me in on who would be attending so I'd have some context when I met them.

The full-day session started well, with about fifty people interacting and energized about the topic. When we broke for lunch, my colleague took a few moments to debrief with me about how specific people seemed to be responding.

"Did you meet the provost?" he asked.

I had previously been a university professor for well over a decade, and my doctorate was in higher education administration, so I felt that I had a lot of experience with provosts. But no one I'd met that morning matched the image I had in my mind of what to expect. "No," I replied with a bit of surprise. "Is he here?"

He laughed at me as he said, "I knew it. You're prejudiced."

Well, that made me uncomfortable—but I became even more so when he pointed out the provost at a table near the back of the room. "The guy in the gray blazer?" I asked. "No," he replied. "The small, quiet Black woman sitting next to him."

He was right. It was embarrassing to be called out as prejudiced, especially knowing that it was true—and I didn't even realize it. It was unconscious. That incident started opening my eyes to the reality of how we make assumptions about others without really knowing them.

### "But I Didn't Know . . ."

Today, we have a term that describes this process: *unconscious bias*. Two words are at work here: *bias* (which is what we decide about someone based on our own limited experience) and *unconscious* (which means we usually don't know it's happening). Here's how it works.

Bias is the brain's way of sorting through input quickly so we don't have to make conscious decisions about every little thing that enters our mind. You meet someone new, and they look and act just like someone from your past. You assume the new person *is* just like your previous acquaintance—but you're probably completely wrong. If you liked the original person, you'll feel positively toward the new person. If you didn't like them, you'll be suspicious of the new one.

When we meet someone we have a lot in common with, we tend to prefer them over people who are *less* like us. This is called the *similarity effect*, which can be dangerous. Dr. Matt Grawitch says, "When we encounter new people . . . we don't know anything about them beyond their physical appearance. This can lead us to have a bias *toward* people who appear more like us (e.g., age, race, sex, body type) or *against* people who appear to be different from us in appearance."[1]

Bias means that we form opinions about people based on our first impressions—how they look and how they act. We don't have any data to make an accurate decision, so our brain starts with what's familiar.

What happens in your head in each of these situations?

- Someone cuts you off on the freeway without signaling, causing you to quickly apply your brakes to keep from hitting them.
- A person standing at the off-ramp is holding a sign that says, "Lost my job—please help."
- The person you're assigned to partner with on a work project is twenty-five years older than you—or twenty-five years younger.
- The heaviest job applicant has the best résumé.

Isn't it fascinating that without any interaction or knowledge about the other person, we nevertheless form an opinion about their character and their competence.

Bias by itself isn't bad, because it's part of human experience. It's a way of protecting us from possible physical danger or helping us avoid business deals that just don't sound right. The key is to recognize what we're doing—moving that bias from "unconscious" to "conscious." When we recognize what's happening, it's much easier to make choices that don't harm others.

*I'm not biased against anyone*, we think. That's the problem with unconscious bias—it's *unconscious*, so we don't know it's happening.

Based on the events that have taken place in society in the past few years, we're much more aware of these issues than in the past. In the workplace, we watch ourselves to keep from discriminating against someone based on their personal attributes and instead work to have an accurate view of their professional merit. We get it. It's easier to recognize our presuppositions when it comes to "big" issues like race, gender, physical abilities, religion, and so on.

*But what about introversion?*

Do people have unconscious bias against introverts?

## Introvert Bias in Real Time

Training developer Julia Carter suggests three common work-related examples of negative unconscious bias against introverts: interview assessments, training courses, and brainstorming in meetings.[2]

### Interview assessments

Prospective candidates are often given a battery of assessment experiences that focus on group discussions, taking initiative, making quick decisions, and contributing quickly in a group meeting. None of these are natural to introverts, so we're being measured for extroverted abilities. A fair assessment would also include a reflective component where applicants are given a task, then provided time to research, listen deeply, exercise empathy, and express well-thought-out ideas.

"The extrovert may have the initial idea," Carter writes, "but it's often the introvert that makes it work."[3]

### Training courses

Typical seminars often rely heavily on activities like icebreakers and instructions to discuss a concept with one or two other people. "Don't leave nearly half of your audience battling a desire to run away," Carter says.[4] Introverts need a process that allows us to contribute without pressure. We need time to respond, not to feel penalized for taking time to think before answering.

### Brainstorming in meetings

These events usually pull the energy from the extroverts, who contribute ideas quickly and with the most volume, which leaves the introverts at a loss to make reflective contributions. Such sessions have value but can draw the best from introverts by encouraging participants to think and submit new ideas after the meeting has ended.

Unconscious bias toward introverts can show itself in both positive and negative ways. Positive bias could include things like:

- Introverts might be given more important assignments if leaders assume we're hard workers.
- If people notice that introverts don't talk as much, they might automatically assume we're deep thinkers and possibly more intelligent.
- Leaders might put introverts on an important team (but this could also be because the leader thinks we'll be less likely to critique the leader's ideas).

On the negative side:

- People might exclude introverts from groups because they perceive us as arrogant and uninterested in what others think.
- When introverts don't say much, others might assume we're not as smart, we don't have anything to

contribute, or we don't understand—so we might be overlooked for participation on an important team project.

- Some people might be hesitant to connect with introverts because they think it takes more time and work than connecting with extroverts.

### The Treasure Hunt

You're in a team meeting with both your introverted and extroverted colleagues. The extroverts are thinking quickly and talking, bringing energy to the discussion. The introverts are listening and processing, not saying much. The extroverts are more visible, and the introverts are less visible. An outsider could assume that the extroverts have all the good ideas and the introverts don't have anything to contribute.

That's where unconscious bias comes into play. Observers don't realize that they're assuming the extroverts are making a bigger contribution than the introverts because the introverts are easy to overlook.

If we all became aware of our unconscious bias, we could turn it into *intentional appreciation*. We could fully appreciate the role of the extroverts and their contributions, as well as be intentional about seeking out the uniqueness of introverts. We could recognize that everyone has a treasure chest of unique contributions, no matter what their temperament. With extroverts, the treasure chest is close to the surface, and everyone knows where to look. With introverts, it's often buried deeper and hidden—and we can "mine" these resources. In both cases, overcoming unconscious bias means we put aside our assumptions and go on a treasure hunt.

In the workplace, tapping the resources of both extroverts and introverts impacts the success and bottom line of the company. When we take the initiative to demonstrate our unique contributions, management and other team members can recognize how much value has been overlooked. Once they've witnessed the value introverts bring, they'll be more likely to see those contributions as a rich addition to the team.

Executive leadership coach and podcast host Kathy Caprino chronicled her own transformation from unconscious bias against introverts to intentional appreciation:

> I didn't recognize introversion for what it truly is, and I had a negative bias against it because 1) it is very different from my own way of operating, and 2) I mistook extroversion for being able to think and analyze quickly, knowing and being on top of what you're talking about, and being a strong leader and manager. . . . I began to focus more intently on my own biases against introversion, and saw that they were rampant. Where I used to see staff members or colleagues as "not able to think on their feet," or "so quiet that it hurts them," I now see the keen power of their minds, their intense creativity and brilliant ideas, along with their ability to comfortably share power with others rather than needing to put their mark on other people's ideas.[5]

## Flipping the Script

The place to start is to recognize the prevailing myths about introverts in the workplace, then have intentional discussions around possibilities. If you and your introverted coworkers seem to be overlooked, develop some genuine, intentional relationships with a few extroverts. If nobody is considering you for a leadership role, exhibit your leadership abilities in simple and visible ways in your current circle to show your value. If people think you're too quiet to have anything to offer, counter it with genuine, visible contributions that bring value to your team.

As an introvert, your specialty is connecting with the smallest groups possible—especially one-on-one. Connect with an extrovert you know well and share your ideas. Get their input and see if they can catch your passion. They might become the catalyst for changing everyone's perspective.

It's time to take an extrovert to lunch!

4

# Myth Busters

They say that there can never be two snowflakes that are exactly alike, but has anyone checked lately?

Terry Pratchett

What does unconscious bias look like?

In school, most introverts know what it's like to be graded by extrovert standards. It's common for a college professor to feel justified in preparing students for the "real world," which means more than just academic prowess. We've all experienced the class where a significant portion of the grade is based on class participation, demonstration of leadership skills, and taking initiative to contribute to every discussion—whether students have anything of value to say or not.

Because of that, most people have been unconsciously trained to believe two things:

1. Extroversion is the key to success in any business environment.
2. If a person isn't an extrovert, they won't succeed.

That perspective has led to a series of common myths about introverts, making the flawed assumption (unconscious bias) that we are "second-string players." We're part of the team but don't get to play much. We mostly fill in when the first-string extroverts aren't available.

What do people think when they encounter an introvert? And what's the truth they're not recognizing? Let's look at six common myths and six lesser-known truths to see how many of them sound familiar, especially in a business setting:

## Six Common Myths

### 1. Introverts are unfriendly and don't like other people.

We might seem aloof, but introverts usually like people as much as extroverts do—just in smaller doses. We usually prefer connecting with a few people deeply to interacting with larger groups. Our strength is to reflect on ideas before sharing, not to jump in with whatever ideas pop into our heads. In a large group, we listen—then we take time to process alone or with one or two others about what we heard.

Once we've found a few close friends, we tend to be fiercely loyal to them. We like others but do our best work with those few highly trusted colleagues.

### 2. Introverts can't be leaders.

It's true that most managers and executives are extroverts (one study found it was about 96 percent), but that doesn't mean they're more effective than introverts.[1] There are advantages for an extrovert in leadership, but equally as many advantages for an introvert.

Wharton professor and author Adam Grant found that both introverts and extroverts could be highly successful as leaders, but with different types of employees. Extroverted leaders work well with more passive employees who need direction, while introverts do great leading more proactive employees, "validating their ideas and listening carefully to ideas from below."[2]

### 3. Introverts aren't good in certain professions like sales, top management, or public speaking.

Anytime I encounter a high-energy salesperson, my defenses go up. I don't mind them being friendly, but my first thought is, *They're pretending to like me so I'll buy from them.*

Sounds unfair, right? It probably is, but it's a perception from a lifetime of experience. If they talk fast and lay out logical reasons before I have a chance to process, I feel intimidated. They're assuming that an extroverted approach will convince me when the opposite is usually true.

Some professions tend to use more of the skills of an extrovert, so an introvert needs to learn how to operate in that arena. If they really have passion for that field, they can find creative ways to excel using their natural temperament.

Pick a profession for the energy it gives you, not just for the money.

### 4. Introverts aren't good at networking.

As a young introvert, I wanted to succeed in business. I knew that building relationships was the best way to make that happen, because that's what I saw in the successful people I knew—and they were extroverts. I studied how they did it by reading books like Harvey McKay's *Dig Your Well before You're Thirsty* and Keith Ferrazzi's *Never Eat Alone*. Those books were motivating, and I gleaned tips and techniques for networking that sounded powerful, such as:

- "You do not get what you want. You get what you negotiate."[3]
- "Connecting is one of the most important business— and life—skill sets you'll ever learn . . . because people do business with people they know and like."[4]
- "We are the people we interact with."[5]
- "There is genius, even kindness, in being bold."[6]

The problem was that those tips felt completely foreign to my temperament, the opposite of how I had been wired. I tried their ideas and made some progress—but it seemed like I was selling my soul to make it happen. If I continued that pattern, I would be living a lie for the rest of my career just to climb the corporate ladder.

Fortunately, I didn't give up. I didn't just say, "Well, that's good for extroverts—but not for me." I learned how to adapt the best suggestions to my own temperament and add them to my skillset. I realized that the instructions were given so extroverts could tap into the best of who they were—and I needed to do the same. The goal wasn't to network in extroverted ways but in introverted ways. The bottom line was to build real relationships with real people. That's something introverts specialize in, and it can make us the best possible networkers— while being true to ourselves in the process.

### 5. Introverts are always "deeper" than extroverts.

Introverts aren't usually big fans of small talk. We can do it, but not for long. Our goal is to get to deeper things, such as the things we've been thinking lately, the challenges we're facing, or our dreams for the future. Small talk paves the way to get to that deeper level, so we'll engage in it for that purpose.

In other words, we prefer "big talk" to "small talk." We're good at both, but our preference is definitely for "big talk."

That's why people assume introverts are deeper than extroverts, but it's usually just a difference of approach. Neurological research has found that introverts and extroverts both feel great after social interaction—but we get that satisfaction with much lower amounts of social interaction than extroverts do.[7] Extroverts get more payoff from the interaction itself, while we take time to process what we've learned from a shorter conversation.

It's like driving to a neighboring state for vacation. Extroverts might want to take the interstate so they can get there quickly, looking forward to what they can do when they arrive. Introverts might take the scenic route because there are treasures to discover along the way. We take different routes but end up at the same destination.

### 6. Introverts like to listen more than talk.

As introverts, we usually don't talk unless we have something to say. But once we've processed our ideas, we're more than willing to share. Extroverts don't mind playing with ideas out loud, so it's not a surprise that we hear from them more often.

We can talk at length about things we're passionate about, but we're careful about how it's coming across. We're watching the other person's response and will usually stop if we're interrupted too often. We put a lot of thought into the few words we say, and it's frustrating when someone interprets our brief pauses between words as a signal to add their own comments.

At the same time, we like to listen—and do it well. We have a natural curiosity about another person's story and enjoy hearing the details. As introverts we tend to listen more than we speak, and it's often tied into how drained we already are. The longer we've been in a socially stimulating situation, the fewer words we have available.

When extroverts see that we aren't talking much, they often interpret that as a sign of discouragement or depression. It doesn't mean we don't want to talk to them; it means we just don't want to talk right now, period. Usually, it simply indicates we're thinking or listening. We talk when we have something to contribute, and that's often something we've taken time to think through so we say it correctly.

Silence isn't a problem for us. It's our happy place.

***

It's tough to contradict longstanding myths. If people believe they're right, they usually don't care about anybody else's opinion.

But just because a lot of people believe something doesn't mean it's true. Society has come a long way in appreciating introverts. In the workplace, we may still experience a bias toward extroverts—which comes from well-meaning people who have no idea they're doing it. That's the essence of unconscious bias.

## Six Lesser-Known Truths

How can we help colleagues discover the truth about introverts? By helping them see what they—and the company—are missing. Everyone's different, but these six truths generally apply to most introverts.

### 1. Introverts don't want to change into extroverts.

Extroverts might assume that introverts would be happier if we just learned to be more outgoing. Simply stated, it's not true or even possible. One study showed that a baby's temperament can be predicted based on their reaction to stimuli at just four months old.[8] In other words, we were born with our temperaments.

As introverts, we have unique skills that we bring to any organization, especially focused around deep thinking and strategy. We're keen observers of what's happening, and we know how to read the dynamics of a group well. We bring substance to any endeavor.

We know where our strengths are and wouldn't want to trade them. Sure, we know we can always refine our conversational skills, *and* we'll always be introverts. We don't need to become more outgoing in order to be good team players. We need to be ourselves.

### 2. Introverts need time alone to recharge.

Where we find our energy is probably the most significant difference between introverts and extroverts. We both need energy to function in business, and we can both do it well. But that energy comes from different places. Extroverts recharge their energy by interacting with others. We recharge by pulling away from others and spending time alone.

It doesn't mean we don't like to socialize. We can be surprisingly social and enjoy it, but it drains us, and we need time alone to catch our breath and refill our tanks. Being alone makes us feel like ourselves again. Author Marti Olsen Laney says extroverts are like solar panels, getting energy when they're out in the open and running low when they're alone. Introverts are like phones with rechargeable batteries—working extremely well in public but being drained by the engagement. We need time away to plug in and refuel.[9]

### 3. Introverts are not loners or shy.

Introverts are often great public speakers and can function well in social settings. We have deep friendships, but with a much smaller circle of people than extroverts might. We'd rather have a few close friendships than a lot of casual ones. It's a matter of quality versus quantity. Building a relationship is an investment, and we want that investment to be a good one. We have a limited amount of energy to invest—it has to count.

Since we understand our energy limitations, we're careful where we use that energy. We're usually not quick to share our feelings, preferring to show how much we care through our actions instead. One introvert said, "Just understand that if you're in our lives, you matter to us. We don't let just anyone in."

### 4. Introverts often prefer writing to talking.

If someone leaves us a voicemail, they shouldn't be surprised if we respond with a text or email. We love writing because it allows us to edit what we say, ensuring we say precisely what we mean. That's tough to do in a live conversation. Research shows that introverts rely more on long-term memory than short-term memory, so it takes longer to retrieve the information and words we need. That's why we might hesitate when we're speaking. Extroverts use more short-term memory, so everything is accessed more quickly.[10]

Introverts think—a lot. Our rich inner worlds and expansive ideas become the fuel for our creativity and our ability to find creative solutions. When we put our thoughts in writing, it makes them more accessible and organized—and clears our head in the process.

### 5. Introverts need time to think.

Introverts usually won't give quick answers. We will slow down while we process or even ask for time to think and respond later. We don't talk about our ideas to explore them; we think through things first so we can share our well-crafted thoughts.

Sometimes in a group discussion, we blank out because we're pursuing our own thoughts. It's not because what's happening around us isn't interesting; it's because what we're thinking about is *more* interesting.

## Basic Differences between Introverts and Extroverts

Introverts like having a few close relationships or being alone, and they love to think. Extroverts like having lots of relationships and love to talk.

Introverts listen more than they talk. Extroverts talk more than they listen. (Though both groups can do both things well.)

Introverts form their ideas through thinking. Extroverts form their ideas through conversation.

Introverts get energy from being alone. Extroverts get energy from social interaction.

Introverts are quiet on the outside but noisy in their heads. Extroverts are outgoing, and their thoughts revolve around relationships more than ideas.

Introverts usually don't like change. Extroverts have no problem with it.

Introverts will talk about themselves with people they know and trust. Extroverts will share about themselves with anyone.

Introverts can concentrate on anything. Extroverts can be easily distracted.

It's tough for us to be creative spontaneously or in a group setting. We listen and observe, think through it on our own, then return with our ideas. Also, we can be paralyzed in a large group discussion; we can hold our own in a small group and can interact much better with one or two others. But our sweet spot is when we're able to think by ourselves.

### 6. Introverts do our best work alone in quiet surroundings.

An introvert is someone who prefers calm, minimally stimulating environments. Some of us have a higher tolerance for a chaotic environment than others, but most of us get an "introvert hangover" when we spend too long in noisy situations, in large crowds, or with new people.

The more secluded we are, the more we're able to focus deeply and produce our best work. We might feel more creative and come up with more unique ideas, and we tend to focus better so we get things done faster. We know how to collaborate on teams but recognize the need to spend quiet time processing when meetings are over.

Many of us get especially drained in a noisy environment. If our work team goes to a crowded restaurant where we have to yell to be heard, our energy drops exponentially. We might visit the restroom several times—not because we need to, but simply to recharge for a few minutes.

When people have unconscious bias toward introverts, they don't recognize the myths they believe unless someone points them out. At the same time, they might be overlooking the truths, which prevents them from tapping into those lesser-known strengths. We can overlook our own strengths as well, especially if we've lived in an environment where unconscious bias was prevalent. We might need to remind ourselves so we're fully aware of the strengths we can bring to the workplace.

Everyone benefits when we see ourselves and each other accurately, challenging the myths and reinforcing the truths. When it happens, we have a foundation for impact.

5

# How to Talk to Yourself

I say, "No worries" far too much for someone who is approximately 94 percent worry.

Unknown

Are you friends with you?

Think about the people in your life you consider as friends. They're the ones you do life with, connect with, and grow with. At some point you found common ground with them, and that became the connective tissue that pulled you together. If you haven't talked to them for a while, there's something inside that makes you want to reach out. When you've been together, you usually walk away feeling stronger than before.

Sure, you have disagreements and times of frustration. But you value them enough to work through those things. When they're discouraged and facing unusual challenges, you don't berate them or come down on them. You encourage them in any way you can because you care about them. They're feeling bad, so you tip the scale toward truth so they see themselves more accurately—and feel better in the process.

And they do the same with you.

There are exceptions, but true friends help each other through the tough times. When one says, "I'm so stupid for doing that," or "I can't do anything right," the other person doesn't respond with, "Yep. You're right. You're stupid and incompetent. In fact, you're also ugly and nobody likes you." A true friend challenges those negative thoughts, describes how their thinking is inaccurate, and points out the positive things that are true that the other person is ignoring. They challenge the lies with truth.

*Then why we can't do that with ourselves?*

Think of the things we often say to ourselves:

*Everybody is more confident than I am.*

*I can't think fast enough in a conversation.*

*I'm too quiet, so I'll never be successful.*

*I can't overcome my habits.*

*It's too late for me to change.*

*I can't overcome the baggage from my past.*

*Nobody cares what I think.*

If you heard one of your good friends say any of these things, you would point out their exaggerated perspective of themselves and move them toward seeing the positive possibilities. You'd acknowledge what they're feeling but then focus on what's true. You wouldn't try to talk them out of their feelings but would empathize and guide them toward a gentler reality. Right?

What happens when we say those negative things to ourselves? If there's nobody around to give us perspective, we believe those thoughts. It never occurs to us that they might not be true, so we don't challenge them—and those thoughts become our reality. We're compassionate to others; why is it so hard to be compassionate to ourselves?

Psychologist Marina Krakovsky describes the most basic level of self-compassion to mean "treating yourself with the same kindness and understanding that you would a friend." She says that "people who struggle with self-compassion don't necessarily lack compassion toward others; they just hold themselves to higher standards than they would expect of anyone else."[1]

Why do we tend to believe all our negative thoughts about ourselves, but we can immediately see the problem with someone else who's doing the same thing?

Someone said, "Never go scuba diving alone." When you're deep in the ocean, that makes perfect sense. If something goes wrong, there's another person to help. Likewise, when we go diving alone into the thoughts that swirl around in our heads, it's easy to end up in a toxic mess with no one to give perspective.

Maybe it's time to stop accepting every thought we have about ourselves as true. Maybe it's time to challenge those thoughts. Maybe it's time to become our own friend again.

## Stop Listening, Start Talking

Because introverts don't like to make a big splash, people around us don't always notice our contributions. And when they don't notice, that's easy to take personally. It becomes a measure of our personal worth. Negative, cruel thoughts begin to surface in our minds. Since we don't challenge them, they become part of our narrative—which directly determines how we feel about ourselves.

These feelings are almost always negative.

Researcher and author Shad Helmstetter explains that through the age of eighteen, the average person has been told "no" or what they couldn't do an average of 148,000 times.[2] Most of it comes from siblings, parents trying to protect us, teachers, schoolmates, work associates, advertising, and the media. They might mean well, but that repetition over the years feeds our brains a negative perspective about ourselves. In fact, research shows that up to 77 percent of everything we think is negative, counterproductive, and works against us. Repetition turns it into our reality.

At the same time, Helmstetter has recorded countless instances of adults who can't remember a single time someone told them "yes"—that they *could* accomplish things and that they *were* valuable just the way they are. Even for those brought up in a supportive environment where their value and success were reinforced, those supportive statements totaled only a tiny fraction of the 148,000 negative pieces of input. What does the brain do? "[It] simply believes what you tell it most. And what you tell it about you, it will create. It has no choice."[3]

Our brains simply do what they're told. The inputs they receive determine the way we think.

If that's all true, *what would happen if we could change the script?*

We've all experienced common situations where we automatically respond to things that happen to us with negative dialogue:

- We trip on a crack in the sidewalk and say to ourselves, "You're clumsy."
- We bang our head on a cabinet and say, "What's wrong with you?"
- We lose our car keys and say, "Again? You can't do anything right."
- Our kids start to exclude us and we think, "I'm useless."

Author Robert Wolgemuth quotes Welsh preacher Martyn Lloyd-Jones, who said, "Have you realized that most of your unhappiness in life is due to the fact that you are listening to yourself instead of talking to yourself?"[4] He suggests that when we wake up in the morning, our earlier thoughts are talking to us, bringing back the problems of yesterday. Our job is to challenge them and talk back to them, countering them with truth.

Most introverts have had the same script of "less than" for so long that we often can't imagine any other script could exist. Our default setting is to respond to every situation with regret over who we are or what we did. A minor mistake in judgment becomes a major source of shame, and we keep replaying it in our minds for weeks, months, or even years. It reinforces our role as a failure.

There's a better way.

## Creating a New Script

Rewriting the script involves two perspectives:

1. Realizing that the old script no longer serves us.
2. Recognizing that it's possible to replace that script with a new one.

Let's say you find yourself at a loss for words when your boss calls on you during an important meeting. You simply need a few extra seconds to formulate your thoughts. But since you don't respond, your boss simply moves to someone else.

*Well, that's painful,* you think. You feel embarrassed and humiliated. You assume that everyone in the room is focused on your failure to contribute, and you've already decided what they're thinking: *What a loser. Why are they even on our team?*

Could it possibly get worse? Absolutely—by reliving the whole experience over and over. Each time the painful situation comes to mind, you reinforce your negative view of yourself. You're not just reviewing what happened; you're reinforcing what you decided everyone is thinking about you. You're not wondering how they feel about you anymore; you believe it—and it gets worse over time. You're embarrassed to show up at work the next day because you "know" what everyone is thinking.

In reality, they're probably not thinking about you at all. The event was simply a blip on their radar, and they all remember times when something similar happened to them as well. It was a moment of humanity, and they moved on. If you can't move on, the event has turned into a roadblock for your emotions, self-esteem, and future contribution.

How do you move on? By feeling your feelings but also challenging them with truth. *That was horribly embarrassing, and I hated looking foolish in front of my boss and colleagues. But I'm not going to live in that situation, reviewing it over and over. How they feel about me isn't nearly as negative as I think it is. It's over, so it's time to move on.* Whenever you catch yourself starting to replay the event, use that as a trigger to "turn off the video" and direct your attention to whatever you should focus on next.

Don't ignore your feelings but acknowledge them, feel them—and challenge them with truth. That's the only way you'll be able to move ahead and keep from wallowing in regret. If you suppress or ignore those feelings, they'll keep coming back to haunt you with even more power.

## How to Let It Go

What about the negative self-talk we've had for our entire lives? Can we simply decide to think differently moving forward, and everything will magically be OK? That would be like deciding to reverse direction in an ocean liner crossing the Pacific. The captain doesn't spin the wheel and cause the ship to immediately turn around. It's a gradual process, and it takes time—but small movements done consistently get the desired results over time.

"Holding on is believing that there's only a past; letting go is knowing that there's a future," says author Daphne Rose Kingma.[5] We know this instinctively, which is why songs such as "Let It Go" from *Frozen* have such universal appeal. Change happens moment by moment, decision by decision. We make those decisions repeatedly until we form a new habit.

Wharton professor Adam Grant describes the necessity of pursuing a new direction: "The point of reviewing your mistakes isn't to shame your past self. It's to educate your future self. Rumination is recycling old thoughts about what went wrong. Reflection is looking for new insights on how to do better."[6]

"You can't undo last year," he says. "You can improve this one."[7]

It's tempting to hold a vision of the perfect person we'd like to be in the future, then scold ourselves for not being there yet. The first step in changing our self-talk is to become keenly aware of each time we speak harshly to ourselves, then use that as a trigger to challenge that thought and replace it.

When you catch yourself speaking unkindly to yourself, try saying the words out loud with the appropriate level of feeling. Listen as though someone else were saying it to you in that same tone of voice. How would that feel? Then say, "You can't talk to me that way!" in the same voice you'd use with someone who was treating a friend of yours harshly. This is standing up for yourself in the most appropriate way possible.

Clinical psychologist Steven Hayes likens these interactions with yourself to unruly passengers in the backseat of a car you're driving. "Sure, you hear the noise and ruckus behind you, but you keep your attention focused on the road ahead."[8]

This applies in every situation but is especially relevant in the workplace, where you're bantering with coworkers and customers all day long and evaluating yourself based on what they say to you (or what you think they're thinking about you).

Sound artificial? Not really. It's a way of catching yourself when you're not treating yourself with the respect you deserve. It's a way to take control of your thoughts so you can replace them with thoughts that are honest, true, and encouraging. For an introvert, it's a way to change your mindset. Change your thoughts, and it changes your choices—which can change your life. That's the foundation for learning to thrive in an extrovert world.

## Tips for Reconstructing Your Self-Talk

When you catch yourself saying things that reinforce a negative, what practical steps can you take in those situations to move forward?

Consider these options:

- *Say "stop."* As soon as you catch yourself thinking something negative about yourself, counter it forcibly by saying "Stop it" out loud. Say it in the same way a good friend would after listening to your negativity until they're finally fed up and say "Stop it." It's a personal intervention to break the downward spiral that can be hard to escape.

- *Surround yourself with positive people.* Research has shown that hearing the way other people talk about us affects what we say to ourselves—whether positive or negative. This isn't "positive thinking" where we ignore reality; it's spending time with people who will speak truth into our lives to counteract our negative self-talk.[9]

- *Use second-person pronouns in your self-talk.* Instead of saying, "I should stop dwelling on that mistake I made," instruct yourself with the word *you.* "You need to stop dwelling on that mistake you made. It's over, so move on." Clearly tell yourself what to do instead of just hoping you'll do better next time. Think of what you would tell someone who asked, "What do you think I should do?" Your response to them is what you should say to yourself. That's what athletes do to ensure top performance, and it's a technique you can use as well.

- *Let your passing thought pass.* When you catch a negative thought, don't keep it as a pet where you feed it and nurture it and play with it. Realize that it's a thought just passing through your mind, not truth—so let it pass all the way through so it doesn't get stuck.

- *Look for simple solutions that tap into your unique temperament and skills.* Everyone needs to stretch in order to be successful in life and work. You don't need to become something you're not; just learn how to do the uncomfortable thing in a way that utilizes your strengths. For example, if cold-calling is part of your job, warm the prospect up with a well-crafted email to set the stage for your call. When you're attending a meeting or conversation where you're not in charge, build your own agenda so you're prepared.

## The Keys to Powerful Self-Talk

Have you viewed your introversion as a liability? *Stop it.* Decide what's true and positive about your introversion, and say it to yourself often.

- *People like me because I'm easy to get along with.*
- *I'm creative and curious, and it makes me good at exploring.*
- *I think deeply, so I'm good at solving problems.*

- *I'm a good listener and know how to build deep relationships.*
- *I'm able to focus and block out distractions.*

Repeat consistently.

In an extrovert world, you may not get a lot of affirmation from others about the value you bring in the workplace. But that doesn't mean it doesn't exist. Instead of worrying about what others think, focus on *competence*—becoming world-class at what you do. Be proactive about your career path. Don't flaunt your knowledge, just make sure you know your stuff.

Then use your introvert superpowers to become visible and make a difference in the life of everyone you meet. Don't try to make yourself look good; make others look good.

That's what real relationships are made of, and it's how you can make a difference in the world.

PART 2

# THE SEVEN
# MASTER MOVES

Wayne Gretzky never looked like a typical hockey player. By his own description, he said, "I look more like the guy who bags your groceries at the local supermarket."[1] But in the 1981–82 season he scored ninety-two goals, breaking the National Hockey League record and earning the title "The Great One." And today, forty years later, he's still considered the GOAT— Greatest Of All Time.

One journalist wrote, "Gretzky's gift, his genius even, is for seeing. . . . To most fans, and sometimes even to the players on the ice, hockey often looks like chaos. But amid the mayhem, Gretzky can discern the game's underlying pattern and flow, and anticipate what's going to happen faster and in more detail than anyone else in the building."[2] In other words, he wasn't the fastest skater or the most accurate shooter. His greatest strength was mastering the ability to predict where the puck was going to be an instant before it arrived.

It's what we might call a *Master Move*. It was something Gretzky had studied and practiced and mastered until it simply became the operating system by which he played the game. He didn't stop and think about what he was doing; he simply played the game—and his Master Move was his key to massive success.

The book of 1 Samuel in the Old Testament tells the story of the confrontation between David and Goliath. Goliath was a trained warrior—he looked the part, acted the part, carried the weapons of war, and had confidence in his skill in battle. After years of combat, he was still alive—which is a great confidence booster. He had the track record to back up his claims of superiority. He was big and burly and arrogant and loud and intimidating.

David was a shepherd. He had taken care of sheep for years. He had no experience leading people into battle or engaging in combat. He just hung out with the sheep. But he didn't let a giant intimidate him, because he knew his own skill and capabilities.

Put those two résumés side by side, and it wouldn't be hard to guess which one human resources would hire for the position. (Sounds like a job interview with a quiet, thoughtful introvert right after one with a gregarious extrovert, right?)

David couldn't compete against the giant on the giant's terms, but he had developed one single skill that got him both the position and the victory. He had a weapon Goliath would never consider and had developed world-class expertise in using it.

He had a sling—and a few smooth rocks.

That doesn't sound like much compared to Goliath's resources. The difference was that David had mastered his skill. For years, he kept predators away from his sheep, and the sling was his weapon of choice. He probably used his downtime to practice, hitting targets with increasing accuracy. Nobody had his skill; it was his unique Master Move. It became a transferable skill he used with a giant in the same way he had protected his flock.

When introverts become world-class at techniques that come right out of who they are, they won't just survive—they'll thrive. In this section, we'll look at seven Master Moves for introverts. Mastering them in a way that matches our unique temperament will become the foundation for success in any situation. They include:

1. Learning to speak extrovert.
2. Managing energy for peak performance.
3. Creating influence through gentle persuasion.
4. Building trust.
5. Nurturing emotional intelligence.
6. Customizing your work environment.
7. Ensuring success through intentional preparation.

We could jump right into specific tips and communication techniques for thriving as an introvert. But if we don't have these Master Moves in place, our results will be minimal and short-lived. This is an inside-out job, where we build capacity and strength before putting them into practice. We hone these skills until they become second nature.

By building your expertise around these Master Moves, you'll be able to handle whatever comes up in any situation. You'll be on the way to becoming the GOAT in any environment—without compromising who you are.

# Learning to Speak Extrovert

Naturally introverted, selectively extroverted.

Unknown

'␣ve always wanted to speak another language. I'm not sure
why, except I've thought it would be cool to be able to converse
with people in their language. I took four years of German in
high school and still remember a number of phrases, but not
enough to hold a conversation. (My favorite translates into, "I
can't find my overshoes." Living in Southern California, I'm
not even sure what overshoes are.)

The problem was we didn't have many German speakers
in Phoenix, where I grew up, so there was no way to practice.
I figured the only way I'd ever learn was to move someplace
where everybody spoke German—like Germany.

My son, Tim, is fluent in Spanish. His first college job was
in the kitchen of an Italian restaurant in San Diego, and all the
other kitchen workers were Mexican and spoke no English.

He picked up enough to hold simple conversations, since he enjoyed the people he was working with and wanted to connect with them. But he wanted to do more than exchange a few words. He wanted to understand their culture—how they lived and how they thought—not just the language. He saw them as friends.

So he moved to Mexico for about six months to take immersion Spanish language classes, then volunteered there for a few months at a Christian conference center where he could use his skills every day. That's where he met Lucy, the amazing woman who became his wife about six years later. She didn't speak English, so they communicated in Spanish. They came back to America, and he has continued managing restaurants in the San Diego area—which means most of his workers are from Mexico. He has spent most of every day for the past twenty-plus years speaking Spanish.

Why did he become fluent, and I didn't? He had a reason to. For Tim, it wasn't just about learning another language; it was cross-cultural communication, which goes beyond just words. It was about building real relationships with real people, and that meant learning a common language so they could connect.

Suppose you had to move to another country where everyone spoke a different language from yours. What would you do? There are two primary options:

1. You could say, "I don't speak that language, and I don't want to. If they want to talk to me, they'll need to learn my language."

2. You could do everything you could to learn that language as quickly and thoroughly as possible. You'd take classes, talk to people, and practice. You'd learn from every attempt to try to relate to others, and you'd build relationships in the process.

The first one might work for a few days but would become unrealistic as soon as you needed to get anything done. They don't know you, so there's no incentive for them to make the effort to learn your language.

The second one is the logical alternative. You'd start small, learning the most important words and phrases for survival such as "Good morning" and "Thank you" and "Where is the restroom?" People would instantly recognize that you're trying, and most would appreciate the effort. By necessity, you would gradually learn the language. By using that language often, you'd come to understand the culture and learn to communicate.

Being conversant in another language is a distinct advantage for living in another country. As introverts, our first Master Move for living among extroverts is to become bilingual—to learn to "speak their language."

## Learning to Speak Extrovert

The data vary, but most research says that up to 50 percent of the US population leans toward the introvert side, and the other 50 percent leans toward the extrovert side. Obviously, there are varying degrees of introversion and extroversion, but there are a whole bunch of people leaning in either direction. Also, most people aren't pure introverts or extroverts all the time. An introvert might prefer being quiet and working alone, but this gives them the confidence to speak up in a meeting. An extrovert might hold back from saying what they're thinking in order to receive the ideas of others.

As an introvert, your daily life in society is an exercise in cross-cultural communication. In the same way a foreign nation has a unique culture, an introvert in America is living in a country where the national language is "extrovert." Let's look at our two "foreign language" options again, tailored to temperaments:

1. You could complain that people don't see the value introverts bring to the world and complain that they need to wake up and recognize it.
2. You could focus on learning the language of extroversion as quickly and thoroughly as possible. You'll never become an extrovert, but you'll be able to communicate in a "second language." In the process, you'll learn to understand their culture, care about them, and respect them for exactly who they are without irritation.

In other words, if you choose option 2 you'll be more than bilingual; you'll learn cross-cultural communication so you can build genuine, respectful, and rewarding relationships.

*Why should I be the one making the effort?* you think. *Shouldn't it go both ways? Why can't extroverts make the effort to understand me?* Yes, that would be great. But we're the ones who are feeling the pain, not them. We have the incentive—and the payoff.

Nelson Mandela said, "If you talk to a man in a language he understands, that goes to his head. If you talk to him in his own language, that goes to his heart."[1]

Just like my son works all day with people who speak a different language, we go through each day surrounded by "nonintrovert speakers." The only way we can connect is to take the initiative and make the initial effort (instead of expecting it from them).

## What's the Payoff?

"Learning to speak extrovert sounds like a lot of work," you say. "Is it worth the effort?" That's a fair question, one I've asked

## What Words Mean

Learning the language of extroverts is different from learning a foreign language. In this case, we recognize the words we're hearing, but the speech patterns being used are different:

- Extroverts tend to use a lot of words to say something. Introverts tend to be concise and use fewer words to make a point. Listen to the "many" words and see how you might translate them into "few" words.
- Extroverts use more abstract language: "That video was really excellent." Introverts use more specific language: "The last point in that video was really eye-opening." If an extrovert says something was "excellent," ask them to go deeper: "What was it that made it so excellent?"
- Introverts use more qualifying words such as "maybe." An extrovert says, "Let's go get some food." An introvert says, "Maybe we could go grab a sandwich."
- Extroverts use more words about relationships. Introverts use more words about situations or information.
- Put introverts together in a room, and they'll try to solve a problem: "I have to get a different car because gas prices are so high." Extroverts focus on topics that are interesting: "I'd love to go fishing," or "I wonder what stores are going to be in that new mall when it's finished."
- Extroverts are more focused on simply enjoying life. Introverts want to know what's happening below the surface with most topics.
- Extroverts tend to use plural words: "We're in a good place." Introverts stay singular: "I'm enjoying this event."

Pay attention to everything an extrovert says but assume they might mean something different. If you're unsure, don't hesitate to ask for clarification.

myself about learning another language. I enjoyed my high school German classes and would love to speak the language well. If I were moving to Germany, I'd have the incentive. But unless something changes, I probably won't pursue it. With the limited time we all have in life, we have to choose what outcomes we want so we can put our energy toward those ends. For me, that won't include learning German.

But as I thought through this, I realized that I *have* spent my life learning a foreign language—the language of extroversion. I live in a world where most people are fluent in extrovert. I've studied the language of extroverts but also gotten to know them intimately because I work with them daily. I've studied their passions and drives and wiring and culture. I've become fluent in extrovert—but it will always be my second language.

I've taken the time to learn how to live in an extrovert world without becoming one. I make choices about the words I use and the way I approach them, based on what's important to them, not just to me. Learning their language has opened the door to building relationships with some amazing people I might have overlooked in the past.

There are plenty of other benefits for an introvert to learn another language as well, whether it's a foreign dialect or a different temperament.

### We become more observant.

When we can't communicate with words, we become more observant of another person's facial expressions, body language, and subtle gestures. We need those cues to connect, and we begin to look for patterns we can recognize. My wife and I did that with our daughter-in-law, Lucy, when she first came to America. We didn't know her words, but we were able to see her heart by just watching and spending time with her.

An introvert's natural sensitivity to what's happening around them is a perfect tool to use in making such connections.

### Our problem-solving skills improve.

Cross-cultural communication isn't a matter of following five steps, checking them off, and seeing permanent results. We learn words and phrases that work in a different language and try them out. Then we watch the reactions of others to see if we used them correctly. If we didn't, we figure out where the communication broke down, then try saying it differently. It takes time and effort to sort through the options. Every time we repeat that process, we gain more skills in finding the best solutions.

That's what Lucy did with our family when she started learning English. Because it was a safe environment, she was able to experiment and make mistakes without fear.

### We learn our own language better.

We're comfortable with our own language because we've practiced it for so long. That doesn't mean we necessarily use it correctly or well; we often say things that don't come across the way we wanted, and people can be hurt in the process or misunderstand our intent. The process of learning another language takes focus to choose the precise way to communicate something. When we go through that process repeatedly, such care often begins to leak into our own language as well. We find ourselves looking for ways to communicate with more precision.

A few months after my son returned from Mexico, he was conversing with several of his kitchen staff in their language. One of them commented, "Your Spanish is better than ours!" It was a good reminder that since our lives happen through our communication, it's worth learning how to use any language with precision and impact.

### We discover cultural differences.

There are a lot of different cultural groups in the world, but most of them aren't on our radar. If we're actively trying to learn a specific language, we'll automatically begin focusing on the people who speak that language. Anytime we pay attention to another culture, we'll start noticing the differences from our own culture. The more we notice, the more "real" those people become, the more we begin to understand how they think, and the easier it becomes to communicate with them. We notice that they're "just like us, but different." Celebrating differences draws us together.

### Our brain changes.

Learning a second language does more than just make it easier to travel and allow us to watch foreign language films without subtitles. It changes the way our brain works. It helps with speaking and writing (active) as well as listening and reading (passive).

Research has found that the process of learning multiple languages is like exercising our "gray matter"—the part of our brain that helps us think, pay attention, remember things, and process what others say. One study showed that it didn't matter how proficient a person became; the growth in brain function came from the learning *process*, not the result.[2]

## Why Become Bilingual?

Learning to "speak" extrovert is a perfect language choice for introverts. It's more than just knowing what words extroverts use and how they think; the process is ideally suited to our unique skills:

- It taps into our natural listening abilities.
- It forces us to focus on what the extrovert is saying, so it takes the attention off us and puts it onto them.
- It's easy to approach an extrovert with intentional questions and a prepared mental agenda since they generally

welcome the chance to interact with someone. (We don't have to worry about intruding.)

- We can tap into all our best strengths when we start the conversation.
- We don't have to pretend to be something we're not (an extrovert), and we can simply be ourselves in the presence of another person. We're usually the one that feels uncomfortable—not them. We can converse without second-guessing their reactions.
- The simplest conversation is the easiest way to break into an extrovert's culture. It's a little like parachuting for the first time; the toughest moment is jumping out of the plane—but it's a whole new world once we've jumped.
- Introverts are natural at exploring, so we don't have to come with a list of topics. We can ask questions, listen well, and follow up naturally.

## How Do We Do It?

There are many things we can do as introverts to make the learning process easier:

- *Take small risks.* Think of something we can do that's slightly uncomfortable and test it out. After we've done it a few times, it won't feel so risky, and we can try something else. For example, we can ask an extrovert for a simple piece of information: "I notice you've got an agenda for this meeting. I must have overlooked where they were being passed out. Could I borrow yours for a minute, just to get my bearings about the day?"
- *Practice often.* Everything gets easier the more it's repeated. We can look for opportunities to ask a simple

question when we encounter someone, such as the cashier at the grocery store, the barista in the coffee shop, or someone we're standing next to in line. Keep it short, keep it simple, and do it often.

- *Read what they've written.* In a work setting, we see if we can find articles our colleague or manager has written on social media or in company newsletters. We can study emails they've sent as well. This will give us a sense of what's important to that person and how they communicate, which will guide our interactions with them.

- *Offer to take notes in a meeting—or to observe the dynamics that might be overlooked.* Taking notes gives us a way to contribute without feeling obligated to share as much. Observing can provide a way for a leader to discover valuable contributions that are being overlooked. They might think the meeting went well because there was so much energy as the extroverts were sharing, but quieter people might not be expressing their significant ideas in that setting. We could even talk to the quiet folks after the meeting to get their ideas, then collate them and provide a summary to the leader. We can see if the leader would ask participants to share ideas they might have after the meeting and make us the point person for collecting them. Then we send out an email reminder a couple of days later.

- *Give up perfection.* Introverts tend to relive conversational moments that didn't go well, feeling like others are seeing them as a failure. Focusing on mistakes keeps us from moving ahead and growing. Think of a toddler who falls often while learning to walk; it hurts, but the desire to learn gets them back on their feet repeatedly. As someone said, "If you stumble, make it part of the dance."

- *Remember that everyone smiles in the same language.* We use our smile often; it's like an emotional handshake that finds the common ground we have with others.

## Take the First Steps

It's the process that counts, not the result. No one can become fluent in another language overnight, whether it's a foreign language or communicating with another temperament. That doesn't mean we should give up because it seems like it will take forever. As often as possible, we take consistent, tiny steps and trust the compound effect to produce results over time.

What are these results? We'll have the tools we need to communicate effectively in any situation, without intimidation.

# 7

# Managing Energy for Peak Performance

Introverts don't get ready for a party; they gather strength for a party.

Unknown

Your boss says, "I'm sending you to a time management course." What's your reaction?

Most people think, *I don't have time for a time management course.* They have long to-do lists that never seem to end, calendars that are jammed from hour to hour, and never-ending demands from others. It's like they're surrounded by a pile of stuff they have to do, yet it never gets smaller, no matter how much they get done.

That's why "time management" usually has a negative connotation for most people, even if it seems like it could be helpful. It feels related to being stressed, feeling overwhelmed, having a lack of control, and being at the mercy of what other people want. In a work setting, we think, *Well, they're paying me . . . so I just have to try to get it all done.* We don't see any way out, so we agree to go to a time management course in hopes that we can find a solution.

I've taught time management for over three decades, and I can assure you it's not the solution. Why? *Because we can't possibly do it.* Time management is an oxymoron, because time can't be managed. We can't get more of it, we can't store it up, and we've got the same amount as everyone else on the planet.

So, why do some people get so much done, while others don't?

The only things we can manage are our *choices.* If we have the next ten minutes available, we can choose what we do with that time. We could watch a video, prepare a snack, or go for a short walk. We could converse with a coworker, outline a project we'll be starting, or send an email to a client. We're the only ones who determine what value that ten minutes has, because we determine what to do with it.

To manage our time, we need to manage our choices.

When we have more to do than we can possibly accomplish, we need to examine all the possibilities and decide where to focus to get the most important things done. Managing our choices determines our results—as well as our sanity and well-being.

### Energy—The Introvert Wild Card

Both introverts and extroverts have the same amount of time and have to choose what to do with that time. But introverts have another variable: *our energy.*

Energy is the primary difference between temperaments. We all use energy in social settings, in the same way a car uses fuel to travel. Extroverts and introverts both have to refuel. And that's where the difference lies: extroverts refuel their energy tank when they're around other people. We refuel by spending time alone.

Consider the popularity of energy drinks. When we're low on energy, it's tempting to grab a can from a convenience store, hoping it will give us the boost we need. For extroverts, an energy drink is a way to continue their fast pace a little longer; for introverts, it's a way to step up to the plate when we're depleted. In both cases, it's a short-term fix. Imagine pumping a single gallon of gas into a car's tank, driving until it's empty, then pumping another gallon and driving, over and over. It's smarter to stop and refuel completely so we can work without interruption.

Refueling looks different for introverts and extroverts, but it might not be obvious. We might watch how extroverts gain energy in groups, then assume we need to do the same. But we're not wired that way. If we don't intentionally find ways to pull away from others to recharge, we'll run out of gas. If we run out of gas, it doesn't matter if we're a Volkswagen or a Lamborghini—we're not going anywhere.

We've all heard the metaphor that diamonds are formed under a massive amount of pressure over a massive amount of time. In business, this image implies that if we want to be successful, we have to be willing to live with constant pressure for our entire life. When introverts hear that, it makes us want to give up and binge-watch videos for the next three months.

A better metaphor for introverts is that bread dough rises when it's given time to rest. Skip the rest or try to rush the process, and we'll end up with a big, dense cracker, not a soft, warm loaf of sourdough. It sounds counterintuitive, but rest is the lifeblood of an introvert. It's not about being lazy and unproductive when we could be getting something done; it's the very source of the energy we need to succeed.

If that's true, rest needs to become a top priority.

That's why it's counterproductive for us to pretend we're extroverts just to survive at work. We can't just copy an extrovert's actions and attitudes; we would have to copy their energy. If we did that, we'd be draining our own energy away.

Managing energy isn't optional for an introvert; it's critical for both surviving and thriving. That's why it's the second Master Move for success in the workplace—or any area of life.

## Getting Better Mileage at Work

Think of the work situations that require introverts to expend energy:

- Attending meetings, especially when we're expected to contribute.
- Going to conferences that have packed schedules and high expectations for participation.
- Traveling overnight for meetings or presentations—which includes airport crowds, flight connections, being places on time, navigating the fatigue from crossing time zones, and the interaction of the appointment itself.
- Having lunch meetings where we don't get our normal break to regroup.
- Interacting with customers who wander in and want to chat with no end in sight.
- Taking constant phone or video calls.
- Going into a break room that is too noisy to get a break.
- Deciding whether or not to go out with a group of colleagues after work.
- Attending team-building events.

- Working from home but needing to be visible to other team members, as well as showing our boss that we're engaged.
- Finding time to focus and get work done in a draining open office environment.

These can all be common expectations in a workplace, but they have the strong scent of extroversion. They're not necessarily bad; they just don't allow for the unique working style of introverts. So, while extroverts can work in that environment without friction, we have to expend an extra amount of energy just to do our job.

We often think, *I just need to get through this next thing, then I'll be able to relax.* We live from crisis to crisis, from challenge to challenge, assuming it'll be better on the other side. The problem is that this messes with our natural ways of working, and we lose our quality of life. We're always stressed in the present moment, striving for a calm, controlled future that never comes.

Most people build their calendar based on their availability. If there's open time, they fill it with whatever others want from them, thinking *Well, I guess I'm free, so I need to say yes.* A better way to decide whether to accept is based on the energy needed and the amount of energy we'll probably have at that time.

For example, if we have a free hour right after three consecutive hours of virtual meetings, it's tempting to plug in another appointment when someone asks us to. A more creative and realistic plan would be to block that hour completely off for some type of recharging activity. It could be catching up on reading through some articles we've been wanting to peruse, clearing out some old emails, or working through a video module of an online course we signed up for. There's no "right" choice, as long as it recharges us. We also put it on our schedule so we can respond to someone's request for our time with, "I'm already booked."

## Energy Choices

What's the key to managing our energy? Earl Nightingale said, "Look at what the majority of people are doing, and do the exact opposite, and you'll probably never go wrong for as long as you live."[1] If we follow the path of an extrovert, we face burning out and living in a constant energy crisis. The key is to challenge those choices, then find new, creative, unique replacements for those choices. It's a matter of realizing we can make different choices, then taking the small steps to put those actions into practice each day.

Consider some of these examples we can use to make "opposite" choices.

### Learn how to say no.

Steven R. Covey used to say, "It's easy to say 'no!' when there is a deeper 'yes!' burning inside."[2] If we're crystal clear on a goal we're passionate about, we'll be able to turn down otherwise great opportunities.

### Get to our calendar before anyone else does.

Planning our week before the week begins—adding appointments with ourselves—keeps us from filling our time with the demands of others. Then we can fine-tune our plan before starting each day.

When we've blocked off time to focus on a project or to give ourselves space to process conversations and meetings, we need to treat those appointments like an important meeting with our boss. When someone says, "I need to connect tomorrow morning at 9:00," but we've set an appointment with ourselves, we can say, "I already have a commitment then, but I've got thirty minutes at 11:00. Would that work for you?" We don't need to explain or justify our reasons; we just say we can't make it.

### Evaluate our energy needs.

Anytime an opportunity arises and we can choose whether or not to accept it, we can resist automatically saying yes. We first evaluate the opportunity by asking ourselves these questions:

- *How much energy will this take?*
- *Will I have that much energy available at that time?*
- *Will I be able to recharge soon after?*
- *Is this the most valuable use of my time?*
- *If I say yes, will I feel energized or depleted by that decision?*
- *Will I feel energized or depleted after the opportunity?*

At times, saying no won't be an option. In those cases, we can begin thinking through creative ways to maximize our energy resources to complete the assignment in a way that will be more energizing than draining. For example, we can plan a time cushion before and after the assignment and little breaks in the middle.

### Stay in motion.

Whether we're working in an office or remotely, we can get up and move on a regular basis. We can encourage ourselves by setting a timer or alarm or wearing a fitness tracker that prompts us to get up and move consistently. It's easy to get wrapped up in an engaging project, but it's critical to keep our bodies engaged as well. This can be walking a lap around the office, going to a restroom on a different floor (and taking the stairs), or leaving your house and walking outside for five minutes.

When it comes to energy, it's not about quantity; it's about frequency. Little bits of movement recharge our brain and re-energize us for work.

### Hide.

If we're in an office setting and people keep interrupting us, we can find another location to work for an hour or so. It might be an empty conference room in another part of the building or a coffee shop nearby. It goes on our calendar as an appointment just like any other important meeting so we can protect the time. We don't have to say what we're doing; we're simply not available.

### Avoid hurry.

For introverts, working under pressure is especially draining. Sure, there will be times when there's no choice because of the demands of a project or critical deadline. That pressure can be overcome by starting our preparation early for each commitment and making a list of steps that we need to take. Those steps go on our calendar, and we protect those times, since they will be key to keeping our energy up for the duration of the assignment.

### Make thinking a priority.

Introverts have the unique ability to think deeply, but it's usually at the expense of responding quickly. Deep thinking is one of our most critical resources, so we must find ways to incorporate it into each day. This is more than just blocking out fifteen minutes for pondering; it means being intentional about leaving plenty of margin in our day so we can be thoughtful about each task.

"But I'm already overwhelmed," you say. "If I try to slow down, I'll be even more overwhelmed." Obviously, we can't put our feet up on the desk and stare at the wall to ponder.

But when we allow even a small cushion of space around our activities and tasks, we'll find that we get better solutions and ideas in less time—because it's the way our brain works. It sounds counterintuitive, but it takes away the constant pressure of urgency. As a result, our energy—our "miles per gallon"—will increase exponentially.

## How to Recharge

Anytime we're interacting with others, we're using energy. If we're in a job with constant interactions (whether in person or virtual), we'll find ourselves on the low end of the energy scale. It doesn't matter if we're a factory worker with constant interruptions or a sole proprietor who can't ignore incoming phone calls. When our energy is low, that is a trigger for us to refuel as soon as possible. Sometimes it means taking a major break, while other times it could just be taking a few minutes.

Introverts can feel especially drained at a social event or conference. If we need an energy boost, we can take a restroom break or spend a couple of minutes outside before jumping back in. For example, it's typical at conference breaks for people to connect with each other before the next session begins. For an introvert, a different use for that break can be as simple as intentionally walking through the crowd without stopping to engage in those conversations. If someone stops us, we can just say "Hey, it's great to see you. I'll be back in a couple minutes." Doing so provides that important physical movement as well as a chance to pull back from conversation in preparation for the next encounter.

As introverts, we can consider some of these ideas:

- We don't compare ourselves to extroverts and how they engage with others. We're not them, so we must learn to be ourselves and capitalize on our strengths.

- We never see downtime as wasted time. It enables us to function at our best.
- We make an energy budget, deciding from our own experience how much energy we have to give. Then we stick to that budget.
- We figure out what activities recharge us and do more of them.
- We schedule enough "alone time" so we don't end up with a social hangover.
- We avoid noisy, crowded places whenever possible. We save our energy for things that matter instead of letting it dissipate through background noise.
- If we stay out late, we don't schedule anything early. If we have something scheduled early, we don't stay out late.
- We build as many individual conversations as possible to get things done so we don't find ourselves in larger group discussions as often. When we take the initiative to set up meetings, it puts us in control of when we meet, how long, and where—so we're not at the mercy of the choices of others.
- We don't work in the evenings—answering our phone or checking our email. We protect our time to refuel for the next day.
- We leave social events early when we sense our energy dropping. No one will notice, and we'll preserve our energy.

## Do the Important Things

Years ago, I heard someone say, "When you die, there will still be things you didn't finish on your to-do list. Make sure you do the important things." That stuck with me, and it's worth considering when we talk about the choices we make in our lives. Your life will consist of the sum of all the choices you made over the years. At your funeral, nobody will care how many sales you made or that you kept a zero inbox or that you won a performance award year after year. What people will remember is how you made them feel.

It's easy for introverts to live an unfulfilled life because we're trying to get stuff done. When we try to do things the way extroverts do them, it robs us of making a unique contribution to the world. We go full speed, figuring we'll reap the benefits when we retire. But in the end, we'll live in that season for fifty years or more with only a long trail of mediocre relationships and a record of success in things that really don't matter.

Don't try to jam more into your life; know who and what is most important to you and focus there. If you live your life with the end in mind, it can help you decide how to live. As professor Sheena Iyengar said, "Be more choosy about choosing."[3]

## Time Isn't Money

Picture a $100 bill. By itself it has no value. It's a piece of paper that's been printed in a certain way. The value comes when you decide what to do with that piece of paper.

- If you use it to go to the movies, that paper has the value of entertainment.
- If you use it for food, it has the value of nourishment.
- If you give it to someone who needs it, you've given it the value of compassion.
- If you add it to your car payment, it has the value of transportation.

## Energy Management Tips

Don't try to get energy the way extroverts do—spend more
    time with just yourself.
Learn to say no to more things.
Schedule restoration time and margin on your calendar.
Do more of what energizes you.
Hang out with other introverts.
Make a "social interaction budget" so you can spend your
    energy without becoming overdrawn.

Time is the same way. There's no intrinsic value in a minute. That minute takes on the value of whatever you choose to do with it.

The difference between time and money is that you don't have to spend your money. You can save it, invest it, or stick it in a drawer. You can't do that with time; you will spend every minute you have. If you don't decide what you're going to use that minute for, someone else decides for you.

Some choices add energy to your life, while other choices deplete energy. If you make choices that only help you become more productive, you might check more things off your to-do list—but you won't make a difference in the big picture of your life. Check marks without meaning are like participation trophies: they look nice, but nobody cares—and there's no impact.

Introverts don't need energy just because we want to hoard it. We collect it so we can use it to make a difference in the lives of others. As Walt Disney said, "I don't make movies just to make money. I make money to make more movies."[4]

It's the journey of a lifetime.

# Creating Influence through Gentle Persuasion

You will never influence the world by trying to be like it.

Anonymous

L ast night, my wife and I went on a date to a very high-end shopping center. We weren't there to buy anything; we just wanted to hold hands and wander through someplace we don't normally go. Most of the stores were ones you might see on Rodeo Drive in Beverly Hills, names associated with wealth and prestige. There were clothing stores, jewelry stores, specialty boutique shops, and elegant restaurants.

Everything was brightly lit, with display windows filled with creatively designed elements to capture the attention of passersby. Each display was so unique, it made us forget the previous one. Every store went out of their way to convince us to come inside: "Hey, check us out. We are amazing. Aren't you impressed?"

It was impressive, and it caught our attention. But as I'm thinking on the experience the next day, there's nothing that sticks out in my mind. I'm not knocking the mall or the stores at all, because I'm sure they have a lot of things that are exactly what some people are looking for. But somehow, they didn't give us any reason to want to buy anything. It felt noisy and cluttered and busy—and as introverts, our favorite part of our date was the quiet drive home after we were done.

This reminds me of social media. Sometimes it feels like capturing attention is more important than saying something of value. Whoever has the best graphics wins the attention contest. People "shout" to have their opinions heard—and if you're not loud, you're not noticed.

Sounds like an introvert's life, right? We're in a world where image (how we come across) is often valued by others more than character (who we are on the inside). We want to make a difference, but it's tough to compete with fake news and click-bait headlines. In the midst of all that, it's tempting to act like extroverts so we can have the same kind of influence they seem to have. But in most cases, it's not really influence—it's simply attention.

## The Impact of Influence

It's tough for us to act like extroverts for very long, though it is possible, and there's a place for it (which we'll talk about later). I love the description given by writer Kate Jones: "For an introvert, staying in an extroverted state for too long is like trying to write all day with your non-dominant hand."[1] It's exhausting.

Fortunately, it's possible for introverts to cut through the chatter and make a genuine difference in the lives of others. In fact, we're uniquely equipped to do that. Our tools aren't the conventional ones like energetic conversations and an ability to be at our best in large groups. We have our third unique Master

Move: *influence*. It can happen gently and quietly with little or no fanfare; it sneaks under the radar to make a difference in a world that's starving for inspiration and truth.

Introverts can have as much or more impact than extroverts through the power of influence. We bring substance to a discussion without pretending to be outgoing, which wouldn't be natural for us. We don't go around telling people what they should do, we just quietly influence them by asking questions, exploring their perspectives, and listening deeply.

If we *direct* someone to do something and they do it, it's obvious how it happened: "I did it because you told me to." But if we *influence* someone to do something and they do it, they might not even recognize our part in it. They just say, "I did it because I wanted to." Influence is much quieter and subtle, working behind the scenes to make things happen—and it's an introvert's power play.

Author Simon Sinek suggests that there are two ways to make something happen: inspiration and manipulation.[2]

1. *Inspiration.* When we deeply understand what another person needs, we meet that need in a way that exactly meets the person's requirements. It takes time, but the impact is lasting. It's an inside-out approach, getting someone to do something because they want to.
2. *Manipulation (or persuasion).* This is when we use words or logic to get someone to do what we want, especially when time is limited. It's a way to get a quick win toward getting something done. It's an outside-in approach, convincing someone to respond because of what's being said.

Introverts specialize in inspiration but have the ability to persuade when needed (with practice). It just takes a different approach. Jones said, "As introverts, we are not well equipped to win what essentially is a personality contest. At these times, we're attempting to play a game of chess when all we have are pawns—the odds stacked against us. In order to win, we need to play a different game."[3]

Most of us would probably agree that we're a lot more suspicious than we used to be of what people tell us. Many of us used to trust people by default. But thanks to social media, BuzzFeed articles, political campaigns, and sensational programs on television, we've come to mistrust what people say in most areas of life. We've heard so much posturing and manipulation that we almost expect people to be exaggerating or shading the truth, even those we know well. As a result, many people find it refreshing when they encounter a voice of honesty (instead of fluff on the surface).

Inspiration is the introvert's advantage; persuasion is the extrovert's strength.

The refreshing part is that this means we both get to be ourselves. We gain the respect of others when we do exactly that and operate through our uniqueness. It takes more time, because extroverts can make convincing arguments that change people's minds quickly. Introverts build deep trust, but it takes longer. Bestselling author and speaker Holly Gerth said, "I now understand that true influence isn't about getting attention; it's about making a connection."[4]

## The Shape of Substance

We've all encountered a salesperson who says all the right things, convinces us that they're deeply interested in us, and makes the sale—then drops the pretense as soon as the sale is made (or we decide not to buy). Everything about the encounter feels contrived, like a movie set that looks real but is only a façade. Sometimes the conversation is so carefully crafted that it feels real, but introverts can sense that it's a hollow shell.

That's part of the introvert's Master Move of influence. We're able to impact others quietly, affecting them from the edges. It's a combination of several unique characteristics:

- *Introverts are experts at paying attention.* Our powers of observation allow us to sense what's really going on in a conversation. Like a human lie detector, we sense when a story is being "spun." Even if we're not doing it consciously, we pick up on subtle gestures and body language and use them to determine what's true. Some extroverts know that's happening, and they're a bit terrified to talk with an introvert. They feel like their motives are out in the open, and they've lost their ability to cover them.

- *Introverts don't have to make an effort to listen; it's our default setting.* That's why we usually have poor eye contact when we're speaking but great eye contact when we're listening. Instead of forming our next ideas to share, we're using all our senses to take in as much information as we can so we understand the depths of what's being shared.

- *Introverts don't speak until we have something to say.* While it's true that we usually aren't big fans of making small talk, we can learn to do it effectively in an extrovert environment—and even enjoy it. In that case, we're using it to make a connection and build a relationship. At the same time, our preference is to listen to others share their ideas, then process that information until it makes sense to us. We're often the last ones to share, but people have learned that what we say is usually well thought through and worth considering.

- *Introverts don't often force our ideas on others.* That can be a liability, because our thoughts are often the very thing that needs to be included to arrive at a creative, workable solution. Extroverts often keep the energy going in a discussion, but no one considers asking the introverts what we think. That's why it's good for us to learn some of the basic skills needed to inject our ideas in a way that's well crafted and comfortable. (We'll cover those skills later.)

Introverts can use our unique skills to influence others at the highest level. We can feel frustrated when random ideas are tossed around that haven't been thought through in depth, like eating chips and queso until everyone feels too full to eat the healthy stuff. The key to this high-level influence is to recognize the value of what we have to offer, then find introvert-friendly ways to make those ideas heard.

As author and professor Jeff Hyman said, "Quiet people often produce the loudest performance."[5] We get to be 100 percent ourselves—but not to use that as an excuse to not contribute. It can become the base by which we grow into new skills that can make us visible in conversations.

Introverts use our natural ability to inspire others to do things because they want to. The skills of persuasion are more natural for extroverts, but we can intentionally learn and refine those skills, using them to convince others to take action.

## Strategies from Your Sweet Spot

Your power for influence as an introvert comes from the things you do naturally well. Consider these ideas for making an impact.

### Listen, then think, then respond.

We influence people when we listen to them because it's such a rare experience. It says to them that someone values their thoughts enough to pay attention. It becomes the catalyst for people to hear your thoughts because you took the time to hear theirs.

The pattern starts by listening carefully and deeply. Ask clarifying questions without adding your own ideas, and even write down what they say because you value their thoughts. Second, review what you've heard as you add structure to your conclusions. Once you've formulated your ideas, take the third step of speaking up and sharing.

That third step will be the most uncomfortable, but it's the one that takes the ideas in your head and puts them out where others can benefit. That's essential for making an impact and will position you to be known for providing valuable input. If an idea stays in your head, it might be a great idea—but no one knows. If you take the risk to share it, you develop a reputation as a valued contributor. People will begin to see you in that role and will look forward to your rich insights.

### Learn to speak extrovert, but not all the time.

You never have to become an extrovert, but you do need to learn the language (see chapter 6). If you're primarily an introvert, that's where you'll find your greatest security, comfort, enjoyment, and success. Even though you learn to use your developed skills of extroversion, you don't have to use them constantly. Communicate in your "native language" most of the time, especially by using writing instead of speaking. Use your chosen extrovert skills when appropriate; the rest of the time, relax into being who you are.

### Build a strong relationship with a couple of extroverts.

It's easy to hang out only with other introverts. But real strength in business comes when an introvert and an extrovert can combine their complementary strengths, working together with high respect. The most powerful partnership I had in my previous corporate job was with an extrovert who was my polar opposite. We were both amazed at what the other was capable of, knowing that it was totally foreign to us. We had such high respect for each other that we combined forces and built powerful, impactful relationships with our clients, and we became deep friends in the process.

### Volunteer for assignments that exactly fit your uniqueness.

Don't wait for someone to assign you a task, hoping it will be a good fit. Look for opportunities that will tap into your deep-thinking abilities, writing strengths, and clear thinking—something that can be done quietly and mostly alone—then build the case for taking it on. You'll get to choose the work you do, show initiative in asking for it, and position yourself to work in your strengths and your own best timing.

### The Power in Passion

Whenever I was teaching a multiday corporate seminar, there were always sections I could hardly wait to teach. I knew the potential impact of the concept and had experience with how it had changed me personally. I realized how much it could help the participants once they understood and applied the concept, so it was exciting. It felt like eating dessert in the middle of the meal.

At the same time, there were sections that would be valuable to others yet I didn't have much energy around them. I had to cover them since they were part of the classroom experience, but they hadn't been life changing for me. It felt like it was time to eat brussels sprouts.

We don't always have a choice of what we're involved in at work, and not everything we do will be on our list of favorites. To the degree that it's possible, try to either work on things that match your passion or look for the high points in the more routine parts of your job. Maintain your energy around the less exciting tasks by taking time to recharge as needed.

Work hard to become the best introvert you can possibly be, bringing your uniqueness into all your tasks and relationships.

At the same time, take on the challenge of learning the skills of communicating with extroverts. Don't use your introversion as an excuse; use it as a launching pad for world-class impact and influence with others. Find passion in both the people you're working with and what you're doing, and you'll be able to live in an extrovert world successfully. It's not a matter of learning tips and techniques for smiling at the right time and positioning yourself in a certain way. It's relaxing into who you are and influencing others without being intimidated by them.

## Who Influenced You?

When you think back over your life, who influenced you the most? Who helped you become who you are today? It's probably those individuals who cared about you, believed in you, and listened to you. They usually didn't push their own agenda; those who did probably didn't make your influencer list.

In most cases, the people who influenced you the most were people of character who were genuine. They didn't pretend to be someone they were not; they were fully themselves and didn't play relationship games.

It didn't matter if they were introverts or extroverts. People with the greatest influence are the ones who are the best possible version of themselves and purposefully care about the people around them.

Be an influencer.

Be you.

Nobody can do it better.

# Top Five Strengths and Weaknesses at Work

### Extrovert Strengths

1. Develops close relationships quickly with large numbers of people.
2. Is straightforward and candid.
3. Works well in group settings.
4. Has an ability to remember names and faces.
5. Is willing to help those who need it.

### Extrovert Weaknesses

1. Can come across as abrasive or aggressive.
2. Can be too intense or energetic and turn others off.
3. May have trouble getting work done because spending time with others gets in the way.
4. Might value the opinions of others too much (people pleasing).
5. Tends to not share the spotlight.

### Introvert Strengths

1. Focuses on results over process.
2. Is dependable and detailed when completing assignments.
3. Thinks with purpose.
4. Is a good listener.
5. Thinks before responding.

### Introvert Weaknesses

1. Is not a natural risk-taker.
2. Can be perceived as unfriendly.
3. Might ignore consensus and do what they want.
4. Might feel inferior without reason.
5. Can find it tough to work in groups they don't like.

## 9

# Building Trust

A team is not a group of people that work together. A team is
a group of people that trust each other.

Simon Sinek

Prior to the COVID-19 pandemic, many business meetings
happened in person. If you had a new or prospective client
you wanted to connect with, you'd hop on a plane and visit
their office. You'd dress up, show up, and shake hands. Then
you'd eat their snacks and drink their coffee, or eat lunch out
while you got acquainted. You got to know them through conversations, but the connection came through the subtle things
humans experience only face-to-face.

It was how you started building trust. By being with them,
you could sense whether they were trustworthy or not. You
listened to their words, but your subconscious discerned if
their facial expressions, gestures, and reactions matched. If
they didn't, red flags popped up in your mind.

That environment was especially valuable for introverts. Because of our natural tendencies toward sensitivity and observation, being in person is a perfect way for us to evaluate others and get a sense of what the relationship would be like.

Then, in 2020, the pandemic shifted the whole world from a three-dimensional way of connecting to two-dimensional encounters—through a computer screen. While virtual meetings gave us more clues than talking on the phone, nothing could replace being together in person. At first, everybody tried to remain professional, using realistic virtual backgrounds to convince people they were working in an office building. But when they would gesture with their arms and their hands simply disappeared—or pets appeared in the background—it was a dead giveaway.

At first such video calls felt embarrassing and unprofessional. But over time, people took down the façades and took advantage of new opportunities for connection. "Oh, you have a Schnauzer. Aren't they the best?" We were all in the same boat, and it became our common ground. We were all human. We didn't dress up as much, since we were all working from home.

For introverts, going virtual felt like someone poured molasses into our engine. There were definite advantages to meeting virtually in terms of time and travel expense, and companies began to assume it was "just as good" as meeting in person. But the most valuable resource we have for building trust is those subtle signals that happened face-to-face. With that tool taken away, it is tough for introverts to tell if someone is trustworthy. It's also more difficult to prove to others that we are worthy of trust, because our strength is connecting with someone in person.

I gained a client during the pandemic who I met only virtually for the first couple of years. When things opened back up, I finally met with their team in person for lunch. Even though

I knew them well from many conversations, it felt totally different when we met. I recognized them, but they looked and felt much warmer and real in three dimensions. I felt like I was meeting them for the first time, and our relationship was much deeper going forward.

## There's No Instant Trust

The key element in building trust is the first word: *building*. It's not like stirring instant oatmeal into boiling water and you suddenly have breakfast. Trust happens in a slow cooker, not a microwave.

A doghouse can be built in a weekend. But a seventy-story, high-tech office building takes years to complete. There are too many systems and building materials and processes that have to come together to get the finished result. It starts with an idea, which turns into architectural drawings. Contractors are chosen to bring those plans into reality, starting below ground and continuing story after story until completion.

That's how trust is built. It's not something that's decided on and set into place; it's the result of a number of individual encounters in which people act in a trustworthy manner.

When my family moved into our house years ago, there was an old, wooden deck in the backyard. The boards were rotten, and we were never sure when we might step in the wrong spot and fall through. It never happened, but we were always on edge. Because of our experience on that deck, we didn't trust it. Eventually we tore the deck down. Then we began to rebuild, starting with a solid foundation. Each step took time because we needed to make sure it was done correctly so we could trust the final result. Months later, we stepped out onto our new deck without any worries. Now, several years later, we never think about falling through. We took care in the process, so we have high trust in the result.

Trust is especially important for introverts. We want real relationships with real people, not flashy ones that seem to be lacking substance. Once an introvert decides someone is worth trusting, they tend to be unusually loyal to that person.

Trust is built over time.

The Macmillan Dictionary defines *trust* as "a feeling of confidence in someone that shows you believe they are honest, fair, and reliable."[1] It's the currency of relationships. When there's high trust, decisions take less time because you assume the best intent from others. When there's low trust, everything takes longer because you're analyzing every point of the process; you're not convinced of the other person's integrity.

When introverts trust someone, we start conversations with them. Extroverts start conversations whether they know and trust someone or not. We tend to approach only the people we've learned to trust. If there's low trust, we just keep quiet.

## Why Trust Is Important

Trust is rare today. It used to be that trust was the most important thing in any relationship, and that's still true in the most genuine ones. But we have come to expect that people won't follow through on their promises—or that people will tweak the truth to fit their own convenience. It's unfortunate but common.

Last year, my wife and I visited a car dealership to look at a pickup truck we were interested in. I looked at the window sticker and reviewed the information, noticing that it averaged about twenty miles per gallon. The salesperson said he had worked for the dealership for about eight years and knew the inventory well. During the test drive, he pointed out a number of features that sounded interesting, even remarkable. I asked him, "What kind of mileage will this get?" He replied, "Oh, you'll get about thirty-five miles per gallon on this one."

I didn't challenge him, but I knew it wasn't true. Immediately, I felt that everything else he had told me was questionable. I couldn't trust him. We ended up buying the same model from a different dealership.

I've also noticed that it's becoming more common for people to make promises without following through on them. "I'll have that to you by Friday," they say with confidence. But Friday comes and goes without anything happening—and unfortunately, we've come to expect that. Promises have turned into "filler words," something people say out of habit instead of intent.

When that happens, it's tough to trust those people. If they can't follow through with what they said they would do, it's logical to assume they won't follow through with anything else. It's a dent in their character, and they become someone we assume isn't trustworthy.

That's unfortunate, because while we value integrity, we no longer expect it. The advantage is that when you have integrity, it sets you apart from everyone else. You build trust because others know what to expect.

One of the quickest ways an introvert builds trust with others is to do what you say you will do, repeatedly over time. You'll stand out in another person's mind because it's so different from what they're used to. If something happens and you won't be able to complete a task on time, just let the client know your promise will be delayed. People know that things come up, and taking the time to communicate a delay builds trust. Ignoring it leaves the other person wondering and reinforces the lack of trust. It's a simple but powerful way to maintain the highest level of trust in any relationship.

Sure, building trust is tougher in a virtual world. But introverts function best when we're with one or two other people rather than groups. That becomes an advantage in a virtual work environment, because we can use those digital resources to make real connections online—one person at a time.

## Advantages for Introverts

Introverts can usually build trust instinctively, using our natural skills of sensitivity and observation. It goes both ways as we know how to assess the trustworthiness of others, as well as prove our own trustworthiness to others. *Building trust* is our fourth Master Move because we value truth in relationships. We usually don't trust someone until we get past the small talk and go deeper. It takes time to make that happen, but introverts are generally patient enough to wait.

This Master Move flows from the unique characteristics of an introvert that demonstrate trustworthiness:

- We're skilled listeners.
- We're deep thinkers.
- We're gifted at observation.
- We tend to know ourselves well.
- We're careful and precise in our choice of words when responding.
- We're sensitive, with the ability to pick up nonverbal cues.
- We're creative, so we know how to synthesize the input we've picked up from others.
- When we're healthy, we're not swayed by what the majority is doing and can function with independence.
- We do what we say we'll do.
- We keep secrets.
- We take relationships seriously.

## Trusting Others

Being trustworthy is half of the equation of building trust with others. The other half is *extending trust*. It's easy to watch others to see if they can be trusted or not, but for an introvert to build trusting relationships, it's valuable to assume that others are trustworthy from the beginning. It's the practical application of the "innocent until proven guilty" approach used in a courtroom and eliminates the toxic mindset of suspicion.

For example, how can you build a trusting relationship with an extrovert? By "going first"—taking the initiative to reach out to them, even if it's not as comfortable as keeping to yourself. It's easy to hesitate, wondering if you'll be rebuffed or rejected. But extroverts love conversation and will almost always welcome attempts to connect.

After that first connection, let an extrovert be an extrovert. Sure, they have a different style of conversation, but there can be richness in relationships when you take the time to learn and appreciate their "language." It might feel like you're stepping out of your comfort zone, but relationships are worth the risk—and you'll never know how much trust there will be until you try.

In my last corporate role, I was on virtual video calls throughout each day. Many of those calls were with people around the world from many different cultures and who spoke less than fluent English. At first, it was wildly uncomfortable—probably for both of us. As an introvert, I was grateful when each call ended because it took so much effort to communicate.

As those connections continued and we got past the communication barriers, however, many of those people became close friends. I found that my first attempts to communicate were deeply appreciated because we began to see and respect each other as humans. We explored the things we had in common, which opened the door to explore our differences too.

The result? We built trust.

Pick an extroverted coworker to approach casually with an idea you have about a project you're both working on. If you share your idea with an extrovert, they'll probably want to talk about it. Remembering that extroverts think out loud and share thoughts that pop into their heads makes it easier to converse. Don't aim for a conclusion; aim for a connection.

Make appointments for these conversations. Introverts need alone time to recharge, but extroverts need social time to do the same. If you reach out to them, you're helping them build their energy. It's important to them, even if it's not something you need. When you reach out, you're making investments in trust.

What about your extroverted boss? How can you build a trusting relationship with the person who evaluates your work and influences your salary?

Start with what's important to them:

- They need you to get the job done.
- They need your respect (even if you don't always agree with their choices).
- They need you to represent the team well, both inside and outside the organization.

Then take practical steps to ensure those needs are met.

### Set expectations up front.

Ask respectful, clarifying questions when assignments are given:

- What will success look like for this project?
- What's more important—getting this perfect or getting it done?
- What's the time line?

Getting clarity around the boss's expectations helps you have a structure for meeting those expectations and keeping your boss updated on progress.

### Be intentional about being visible.

It's easy for introverts to try to perform well and assume we'll be noticed. Unfortunately, bosses have a lot on their plates and might not be paying as much attention to our performance as we might like. Take the initiative to offer progress updates around the agreed-upon milestones: "We're just about to finish this first phase of the project—any input before we move forward?" Don't overwhelm them with all the details; just make it a touchpoint so they know you're on top of things. This builds trust because it reminds them that you're doing what you're supposed to do, and they won't need to worry about on-time completion. (This is especially important for remote employees.)

### Surprise them occasionally.

Do more than is expected, showing your initiative. Turn in a project slightly ahead of schedule. Take on a task you know your boss doesn't enjoy doing or come up with a solution they didn't ask you to find. Occasionally send them an honest note of praise for something they did well or appreciation for what you value about them.

## It's Not That Hard

Building trust isn't hard, but it takes time and attention.

- Be who you say you are.
- Do what you say you'll do (and when you say you'll do it).
- Become a person of your word.

Years ago, our church was interviewing a candidate to become the new pastor. In one meeting, they interviewed his wife as well to get a different perspective on what he was like. Someone asked, "What's he like at home?" Her response: "He's the same at home as he is in the pulpit." In other words, she was saying he had integrity.

An appropriate description here is the phrase "without wax." In ancient times, artists would create a sculpture but occasionally might make a mistake in the process. Amateurs would fill those mistakes with colored wax. The great artists didn't. Over time, the phrase "without wax" came to be used to describe anything that was flawless and authentic.

Want to build trust? Be without wax.

## 10

# Nurturing Emotional Intelligence

We can empathize and we can observe without necessarily needing to absorb.

Unknown

Pull out your phone and click on "recent" to look at the names of the last ten people who called you. (If you're an introvert, you'll find them under "voicemail," since you didn't answer the calls anyway.) Then go through the names one at a time and ask yourself, *How did I feel when I saw this person's name on my phone?*

Which name did you find yourself feeling the most positive about, and you looked forward to connecting with them? Did you think, *I haven't heard from them for a long time. I should text them to see if they want to meet for coffee soon,* or something similar? (That's a default response for introverts. We'd rather meet them in person than on the phone, and we look forward to the energy and safety of the conversation.)

Which name did you feel the most negative about, and you hoped you didn't have to call them back? Perhaps you thought, *What's the worst thing that would happen if I didn't respond? Can I just text them a quick response and be done with it?* (That's another typical introvert response for dealing with a person who drains us of energy. We avoid a conversation, preferring to handle it in writing.)

Finally, think specifically about what each person does or says that makes them a positive or negative force in your experience. What sets them apart from everyone else?

There's a good chance that the person behind the positive reaction has what's called "emotional intelligence" (or EQ), and the name that garnered the negative reaction doesn't. Simply stated, EQ is the ability to be *empathic*—to be sensitive to the emotions of another person as well as your own. It's a foundational tool for building and maintaining healthy, vital relationships.

If you know someone with high emotional intelligence, you probably have them on your "nice" list—someone you're drawn to. If you know someone without much of it, they're probably on your "naughty" list—someone who doesn't make your life richer.

Everyone, whether extrovert or introvert, can possess varying degrees of EQ. If someone doesn't have as much as others, they can still practice those skills and improve their EQ. It's usually easier for introverts because of our natural skills of observation and sensitivity. We're used to paying attention to both our own feelings and those of others, so EQ is a natural extension of those characteristics. Introverts value clarity and take time to express our thoughts. Extroverts usually focus more on their words and ideas and expressing them quickly, so paying attention to those details isn't as natural for them. It takes a more concentrated effort and more time, but it's something that can be improved.

Regardless of a person's temperament, knowing how to build and maintain relationships is the key to success in any profession. A person who has great technical skills but poor people skills might be able to carry out their tasks but will never reach the levels of effectiveness they seek. If they're great with people but don't have the competence to excel in their work, they'll eventually be given a new title: *unemployed.*

Someone said that CEOs are hired for their IQ (ability to get the job done) but fired for their lack of EQ (inability to get along with others). I've also heard managers say that when they're interviewing someone for a position, they often hire for chemistry more than knowledge (assuming the applicant has the basic skills to learn the position). "I can teach them how to do the job," one manager said. "But I have to work with them every day, and so does everyone on the team. I want a team that works well together and doesn't have drama in their relationships."

Whether we're introverts or extroverts, success at work comes from (a) our competence in the work, and (b) our ability to get along with others.

The second one might be a little easier for introverts than extroverts.

## What Is So Good about EQ?

Some people assume that extroverts have more natural EQ because they can talk to people and initiate relationships so easily. They might be gregarious and outgoing, but talking skills don't necessarily equate with connecting skills. Look at this partial list of characteristics of people with high EQ:

- They have high curiosity about other people's experiences.
- They listen to understand instead of to respond.

- They're open to change but often focus more on how everyone is responding than to the change itself.
- They're in touch with their own feelings and know how to express them accurately and succinctly.
- They let go of their mistakes so they can learn and grow from them.
- They control their anger.
- They don't hold grudges against others.
- They're likable—probably because they're so genuinely interested in others.
- They respect others.
- They don't seek perfection, which means they don't take forever to get things done.
- They stay calm in stressful situations while analyzing what's happening around them.
- They have an inner sense about what others are feeling, so they handle them with diplomacy.
- They know how to influence people toward a common goal.

Do those sound more like the characteristics of an extrovert or an introvert? Most of them are tied closely to the observational skills of introverts, so we can easily pick these characteristics up and practice them. Extroverts can excel in all of these, but usually because they've made an intentional effort to learn them.

That's why *emotional intelligence* is our fifth Master Move for introverts. It's a natural skill we can move into easily and see results right away. Finding success through this Master Move builds confidence that can affect the way we see ourselves and our ability to be successful in a work environment.

Let's challenge the assumption that introverts all want to be more like extroverts. Sure, some things might look easier for extroverts—and in a lot of ways, it's probably true. But what that overlooks is the satisfaction healthy introverts have about our personal skillset and temperament, with no desire to become anything else. If we need skills to help become more outgoing and better in conversation, we know we can learn and practice those skills without giving up our natural strengths.

Imagine suggesting to an outgoing extrovert that they should learn to become quieter and more reflective. "You should take the next month and just live like an introvert so you can see the value," we might say. "Use that time for self-reflection, journaling, solitude, and doing deep inner work and analysis."

Their response would probably be, "Why in the world would I want to do that? No, thanks."

In both cases, people enjoy the freedom that comes from being the healthiest possible version of themselves—celebrating their temperament and learning to capitalize on it in both their personal and professional lives. They don't want to be like somebody else, but they know they can learn from them. They'll just add new skills to their toolbox and continue becoming the best version of their real selves.

Author Daniel Goleman wrote, "Emotional intelligence is twice as important as IQ and tech skills combined."[1] He suggests that the higher you rise in an organization, the more important EQ is. He also suggests that it's a combination of four key factors:

1. *Self-awareness*—being able to know what you're feeling and how it impacts your thinking and your relationships. It's the least visible but the most important.

2. *Self-regulation*—being able to manage your emotions and choosing how you respond no matter what you're feeling.

3. *Social awareness*—being able to identify empathically with what other people are feeling, share the emotion, and desire to improve their experience.

4. *Social skills*—being able to build relationships through influence, conflict management, teamwork, and inspiring others to maintain healthy relationships.[2]

When we're applying for a job, we submit our résumé, listing where we went to school, what we studied, what skills we have from our work experience, what certifications we've earned, and what we've accomplished for other companies. We know that a lot of people are applying for the same position, so we're competing against them based on these same factors.

We realize that someone will look at all the résumés and triage them based on those criteria. So to get a foot in the door, we emphasize things related to our IQ—our intelligence. We're trying to show that we're smarter than the next person. "Look at everything I've done," we imply. "You should hire me because I have the experience and the competence to do a good job."

But the thing that sets the top candidates apart is what they're like to work with—their EQ. It's tough to add that to a résumé, though, without sounding arrogant or self-serving. Once a person is hired, it's assumed they're qualified to do the job. But how they relate to others is what will *keep* them hired.

In other words, emotional intelligence is more important than we might realize. Most businesses are packed with smart people who beat out the competition to land their job. After they're hired, their ability to relate to others—coworkers, colleagues, customers, clients, and the people they work for—sets them apart (or doesn't). It's our unique competitive advantage in any business.

## What's Your EQ?

The tricky thing about emotional intelligence is that it's tough to know if we have a good amount of it or not. Most of us believe we do, but how can we know? Goleman said that self-awareness is the most important part of EQ; but if we're not "aware," we won't know it's missing.[3] We've all known people who think they have it, but we recognize they don't. *They're clueless*, we think.

Cornell psychology professor David Dunning agrees: "We apply a lot of positive spin to evidence we get about ourselves."[4] He suggests that others are more objective and accurate about us than we are. We all have blind spots that others see and we don't. Since we're "blind" to them, we don't know they exist.

There's only one way to find out what those blind spots are: *we need to find a way to get honest feedback from others.*

That can be challenging for a number of reasons:

- People won't tell us the truth if they don't feel safe with us.
- If we get defensive or make excuses when someone shares what they see, they'll stop sharing.
- The higher we go in the organization, the less feedback we'll get (nobody wants to criticize their boss).
- We're threatened by the possibility of negative feedback, so we avoid it.
- If we haven't had much feedback in the past, we don't know what others' perspectives are. In the absence of such perspective, we make it up and believe it's true.

The best feedback is more focused on observation than opinion. We want to know what another person has seen, not how they interpret our motives. When someone points out the broccoli between our teeth, it's helpful to know so we can do something about it. If they point out that the way we communicate comes across to others as arrogant, that's helpful. It's like looking at ourselves in a photograph and someone points out something we haven't noticed before. It's a blind spot—and once we're made aware of it, we can do something about it.

A manager might tell her employees, "I'm open to feedback. If there's something I'm doing that you don't like, just tell me. You won't get in trouble, and it'll be helpful." When that manager doesn't get any input, she assumes she's doing fine.

However, employees may find it risky to make general critiques of the person they report to. A better approach is to ask for something specific: "I want to make sure I'm listening to your concerns in meetings and not excusing them away. During our next few meetings, could you jot down anything I say or do that makes you feel like I'm not hearing you? I may be doing something and not realizing it." The question involves one specific issue, so the chance of getting a response is much higher and safer.

A 360-degree assessment is also a valuable tool for learning what other people see. It's rare to get honest feedback, and this instrument makes it safe for people to tell the truth because it's anonymous. It's used to let people above you, below you, and beside you share their perspectives about your communication, actions, and performance, and it's combined input so there's no way to identify who wrote any particular item.

One of the seminars I taught hundreds of times in my career with FranklinCovey was their flagship offering, "The 7 Habits of Highly Effective People." It included a 360-degree assessment that each participant would invite others to complete about them as a chance to help them grow and become aware of areas of strength and areas that needed improvement. People submitted their responses online, and participants could print a report to be used on the third day of the session.

I was always amazed at how frightening it was for participants to anticipate seeing their feedback, and we would spend a good chunk of time debriefing in the session itself so they could take a healthy approach to what they saw. For most of them, it was the first time they'd ever received honest feedback about how others viewed them. They feared receiving negative responses, which they had insulated themselves from for years, and were terrified their flaws would finally be exposed.

At the end of the seminar, many participants said it was the most valuable session they had ever attended—not just because of the content but because they were able to get that outside perspective.

When we know the truth and discover our blind spots, we can do something about them. If someone doesn't have a high EQ, they might be sent to human resources for coaching in how to improve their relationships. That could be helpful, but someone with a low EQ will often resist any efforts to change. The best results from coaching come when someone has enough self-awareness to want to improve.

### Can I Buy EQ Online—with Overnight Delivery?

Many books discuss emotional intelligence. Can't we just buy one and read it and apply it? Well, yes . . . and no. Books are a great source of information, but it's hard to get a high level of change by reading one book and trying a few things. We can learn the basics and think through the concepts, but we don't get overnight change from a cursory review of facts.

Seminars and courses are in the same category. While they're valuable for providing insight and understanding of concepts, completing a course doesn't mean we've automatically changed our behavior. It just means we've hit the start button and have a direction to pursue.

Anyone can improve their emotional intelligence, but it's always a journey. It takes time and effort and is often done best in the company of others so there's mutual encouragement, motivation, and accountability. It's like learning to play the guitar. You can learn a few basic chords and patterns of strumming, and your fingers get sore after a few days. It's hard, and people often learn just a little and stay at that level. You find mastery only when you practice those chords and strumming day after day until they become routine, you build the calluses on your fingers, and you learn to play without having to think about every action you take.

With emotional intelligence, you start with the smallest steps and continue over time. Years from now, people will have experienced your EQ as simply a part of who you are. You'll unconsciously relate to others effectively because you've done it for so long:

- You'll go for a "win-win" in every conversation, finding solutions that meet not only your own needs but the needs of others.
- You'll be keenly aware of the emotions you're feeling at any moment, calibrating them to fit each situation while it's happening.
- You'll be dialed in to the feelings of other people without even trying and will use those emotions to guide your conversation.
- You'll pick up on subtle visual cues like body language and facial expressions to know what others are thinking.
- You'll listen for understanding, paraphrasing what they've said to make sure you have it right. Then you'll ask, "What else?" consistently.
- You'll live through a filter of gratefulness, expressing thanks and giving credit to others intentionally.

- You'll be aware of your mindset and know how to choose your thoughts.
- You'll constantly seek feedback from others and use it to grow.

Author and business consultant Ken Blanchard often said, "Feedback is the breakfast of champions."[5] In the same way, we can say "Emotional intelligence is the lifeblood of impactful people."

Success can come because you're smart. Impact comes because you care.

Be yourself and learn to use the Master Move of emotional intelligence.

## 11

# Customizing Your Work Environment

I'm not anti-social. I'm just pro-quiet.

Adam Grant

I arrived early in the morning to set up for the seminar I'd lead that day. I'd worked with this company many times over the years, so I was familiar with the building and knew my way around. We usually met in one of the large conference rooms on the third floor. I checked in at the front desk, got my visitor badge for the day, and headed upstairs.

This time, the entire first floor was under construction. New walls were going in, wiring hung from the ceiling, and the bare cement floors had been reconfigured for a new design.

It was a great company, but its office layout had always been unsettling to me. Each floor was filled with hundreds of small cubicles—the short ones you could see over. No one had any privacy, and they could see and hear everything going on around them. It was busy, it was noisy, it was . . . well, an introvert's nightmare. I often wondered what it would be like to work in that environment, and if those employees were thriving or surviving.

I met my contact in the third-floor meeting room and asked her about the construction. "We're fixing a big mistake," she said. "And it's been going on for years." That sounded interesting, so I kept exploring. "What was the mistake?"

"Years ago, everybody talked about the potential benefits of an 'open office' environment," she said. "The idea was that if people were all in the same big space, there would be more natural collaboration and creativity. People wouldn't have to schedule meetings, they could simply ask a question of someone nearby or walk over to their desk. It was supposed to create an energy about everything people did and keep them motivated. Our executives decided it was a good idea, so we did it."

My question was obvious. "So, should I assume it didn't work?"

"Exactly," she continued. "But it took us years to figure it out. No matter what we tried, none of the benefits the open office promised materialized. In fact, it seemed to get worse."

"How did you figure it out?"

"Nobody was collaborating, and nobody was happy. We did a survey, then we talked to people one-on-one. We realized that we're a creative company where our people come up with ideas on their own. Sure, there had to be some collaboration, but it was the exception. Most of the actual work was done by people who worked best when they were alone, undistracted, and in a quiet environment."

"Bottom line," she continued, "we're a company made up of creative introverts. So, we're changing the layout to create dozens of small rooms around the perimeter of the building where people can go to get some space and focus. We'll still have a lot of the cubicles for now, but people can head for one of those unassigned rooms anytime they need to work alone on something. It won't be perfect, but it's a step in the right direction—and our people are getting excited."

Author Susan Cain cites research demonstrating that "every interruption doubles the time it takes to complete a task."[1] She also says that introverts make more mistakes and experience more stress in an open environment than a quiet one.[2] If a company goes to the time and expense of hiring a solid introvert and then puts them in an open work environment, they're squandering their investment in that employee. It's like hiring a professional chef and making them work in a kitchen equipped with only a kid's Easy-Bake Oven.

You might not work in an open setting, but you might be in a situation where your introversion can't thrive. It might be expectations of others, lack of boundaries for the way you work best, or feeling like you're expected to be more outgoing and collaborative. You might be surrounded by people even if you're not talking to them all the time—so you miss the space you need to thrive. If you feel like you're working in a nonstop carnival, it's time to evaluate.

## Environment Is Everything

It might seem strange to have an entire chapter devoted to introverts' work environment. At least, extroverts might think it's strange. But for introverts, environment is huge. It determines both the quality and quantity of our work, as well as our level of stress and well-being.

Most of this discussion will focus on an office environment. But it applies equally to every situation where we don't get space to do our work alone. You might work in a hospital or factory where there's constant conversation and collaboration, but there is still the need to find creative ways to get space for recharging and producing top-level work.

In an office, we thrive in alone space and wither in open space. We're usually able to work well during meetings and collaboration, but our real work gets done alone. Contemplation doesn't replace collaboration; it precedes it.

Remote workers often struggle when they begin working from home, especially if they're set up in a common area in the house. Finding a small room with a door to use as an office can make a huge difference for introverts because the seclusion keeps our energy level high.

Sometimes in a workplace, that space comes from building trust with others. I have one former colleague (an extrovert) I used to collaborate with almost daily. We learned each other's strengths so well that we could accommodate each other's needs. If she needed to think through how to word a note to a client, she would say, "Do you want to throw around a few ideas, or do you just want to play with it on your own and we'll go from there? Never mind—I know you need to do it yourself first. Text me when you're done." It was refreshing for both of us to have enough trust to be completely ourselves while having such different ways of working.

Making a phone call that others can hear feels like having it broadcast throughout the office. Those "others" are probably ignoring the call, but it feels like there's a constant audience silently criticizing our approach. It's tough to focus on the client when we're wondering how we're coming across to others. I've known some employees who will go sit in their car to make calls so they can have privacy.

To extroverts, this whole discussion might sound silly. For introverts, it's a "make it or break it" consideration. That's why the ability to *customize your work environment* is our sixth Master Move. Get it right, and it lays the foundation for everything an introvert does at work.

Let's talk about how to effect changes within the organization first. Then we'll look at what you can do no matter what environment you're in.

## Crafting a Boss-Centered Solution

The main thing to remember is that if you're struggling as an introvert in your work environment, you're not alone in that struggle. Since up to 50 percent of workers are introverts, we're all struggling with the same things and probably not talking about it. Remember that what's happening isn't your fault, and you're not the problem. It's the environment you're working in.

"But I can't change that," you say. "I can't just go to my boss and ask for a private office." That's probably true, but it doesn't mean you can't begin to have some honest conversations about your needs. As an introvert, you have a unique ability to observe the leaders in your organization and figure out what's important to them. That can help you craft a creative, sensitive way to approach them over time. It will draw from the best of your emotional intelligence as you build an open, honest relationship where you can express your needs in a way that meets their needs as well.

Talk to a few other introverts you work with to see how they're doing in their work environment. You're not trying to build a case; you're simply giving others a chance to share their experience so you and your boss can both have more clarity and a broader perspective around the challenges you're facing. Collect their thoughts, then work toward developing a simple, solid way of describing both the situation and one or more creative solutions. Bosses usually don't respond well to complaining or emotional approaches that feel like venting. By keeping your input objective and factual, focusing on benefits, and offering realistic solutions, the chances of getting your boss's attention increase exponentially.

Here's an approach you could consider:

1. *The need*—lay out how a sizable group of employees are in a work environment that doesn't allow them to make their greatest contribution.

2. *The research*—explain how introverts will thrive and do their best work when they're able to work alone, not collaborating all the time with others. Finding a way to make that happen will increase their contribution substantially—which will impact output, morale, and the financial bottom line. (This can involve key points from your research, such as what has been cited in this book.)

3. *The evidence*—give two or three specific examples of times when the current environment is challenging, plus examples of how changing a few things could positively impact morale and outcomes.

4. *The solution*—provide several options for ways to solve the problem at the lowest possible cost and with minimal disruption.

As much as possible, try to make it a genuine conversation and not a formal presentation, exploring ideas that focus on the benefits of the change rather than just the wishes of employees. Emphasize that you're not trying to "rally the troops" to force a change but that you want to open the dialogue in a way that will bring out the best from up to half of the team.

### Learning to Adjust

What if you can't get the company to make changes to the environment so it's more introvert-friendly? You have two options:

1. *Be reactive.* Give up because it feels hopeless. You're stuck in an environment that's not conducive to the way you work best, and there's no hope of change.

2. *Be proactive.* Learn to accept the things you can't control and to take control of the things you can. Work continually toward creative solutions and find ways to thrive in less-than-ideal circumstances. You can't always control your circumstances, but you can choose your response to any situation.

Let's assume that the first option isn't viable, because nobody wants to resign themselves to a miserable work environment. The second option puts you in a position to look for ways to make appropriate choices in any situation. Sometimes that means looking for another position in a more suitable culture. Most of the time it involves learning to thrive where you are by making creative alternatives.

Consider some of these ideas for taking control of your own environment, whether working in a physical office or from home:

*Find ways to minimize interruptions and distractions.* Use the "focus" setting on a laptop, which cuts off the internet and access to other distractions for a predetermined period. In a private office, close your door.

*Block off focus times on your calendar.* At the beginning of your week, block off a couple of hours each day as "unavailable." Then treat those blocks as appointments that are as valuable as a meeting with your supervisor and protect them in the same way. If someone wants to see you, simply say, "I'm sorry, I have another commitment at that time. I could meet you an hour later for about fifteen minutes, though—would that work for you?"

*Hang a sign when you're focusing.* Let people know that your best work is done when you're focused and you'll be putting up a "focusing" sign to let them know not to interrupt. If they try anyway, say something like, "As soon as I finish, I'll come to your office. It'll be about fifteen minutes." There will be a learning curve, but they'll get used to it.

*Disappear.* Occasionally go to another office, a conference room, or a coffee shop to get some work done. Put a notice on your shared calendar (or a sign outside your door) that says when you'll be back, and make sure you return exactly on time so they'll respect your request in the future.

*Wear headphones.* Don't do this all the time but only when you want to focus. Noise-canceling headphones or ear buds can quiet your work environment dramatically while sending a signal to others that you're doing focused work. Try to limit your headphone period to no more than an hour at a time so people will know you're still accessible.

*Start work early or stay late.* Ask to pick your own office hours if possible, whether at home or in person. If you're freshest in the early morning, show up an hour or two before others arrive and you might get half your day's work done during that time. If you're freshest later in the day, stay after hours.

*Ask to work remotely.* If it's appropriate in the culture and based on your job responsibilities, build a case with your boss for working from home one or two days a week. If they're uncertain if you'll be able to get as much work done without the structure of the office, propose a one-month trial. Agree on how you'll measure performance, then work to meet or exceed those expectations.

*Build a wall on your desk.* If your only option is to remain in a short cubicle with high visibility, make some simple adjustments. Strategically position your desk and monitor. Add a few plants that block other people's view of you, which will give more of a sense of privacy. Don't overdo it; you don't want your desk to look like a tropical rain forest. Just add a few tasteful things that close you in a bit.

*Take frequent breaks.* Where you have control of the length of meetings, set them for fifty minutes instead of an hour. That will give you ten minutes to walk outside or up and down a few stairways to recharge your physical energy. Try to never sit in one spot for more than an hour at a time. If needed, block off those windows of time in your calendar so others will know when you're unavailable for a few minutes and when you'll return.

*Don't work through lunch.* Parkinson's law says that work expands to fill whatever time we've assigned it. If you have an hour to get a task done, it'll take you an hour. If you find out you only have forty-five minutes, you'll get it done in forty-five minutes. It's tempting to feel like working through lunch is the only way to catch up or get ahead. But taking that break clears your head and refreshes your body. Leave the building and take a walk or find a bench outdoors and read for a while. You'll come back with a new energy for the afternoon if you can take a complete break from work. (This is equally important when working from a home office.)

*Type your thinking.* Get in the habit of typing while you think. Thinking is the most creative thing an introvert can do. But if someone sees you simply sitting and thinking, they assume you're not doing anything and will try to interrupt. If they see you typing, they'll be more inclined to wait. You'll probably discover that typing your thoughts helps you formulate and organize them as well.

———

Want to work in an environment that's ideal for your introverted temperament? It's your choice. Create it. Work to make things different. It will help a lot more people than just yourself. At the same time, make the daily choices needed to thrive in any environment, whether things change or not.

Your environment is your "secret sauce" for success as an introvert. Make sure you find ways to make it what you need!

12

# Ensuring Success through Intentional Preparation

Failing to prepare is preparing to fail.

John Wooden

What if I told you that I had a magic pill that would solve every problem introverts could ever encounter in the business world? It would ensure confidence in every situation, guarantee that others see our competence and seek out our advice, and bring respect from every level of the organization. Even better, extroverts would be jealous and want to become like us.

Sounds impossible, right? And it is—but here's something that comes close. It's not guaranteed to fix everything, but it's the simplest Master Move, and it can have a huge impact on almost everything a person touches. It's available to everyone but especially useful for us.

What is this magic pill? Preparation.

If you want to pick just one of the seven Master Moves to implement, *preparation* is the easiest and has the greatest impact. It doesn't take special training or years of experience. All you need is to do it consistently. Preparation overcomes the things that keep introverts from succeeding.

It's simple. If you prepare, your chance of success goes up exponentially. If you don't prepare, your chance of failure goes up exponentially.

A farmer prepares the soil to provide the best possible environment for a bountiful harvest. Without soil prep, the crop might grow but not as well. The seed will have to fight harder just to survive since the conditions aren't ideal. Likewise, if a CEO needs to deliver tough news to employees, preparation evaluates how to present the information in an empathic way to ensure the healthiest response. If that same CEO just talks "off the cuff," the outcome could be completely different.

Some of the most successful people in history built their success around a mindset of preparation. Abraham Lincoln reportedly said, "Give me six hours to chop down a tree and I will spend the first four sharpening the ax."[1] Albert Einstein reportedly said, "If I had an hour to solve a problem, I'd spend fifty-five minutes thinking about the problem and five minutes thinking about solutions."[2] Dr. Stephen R. Covey used to say, "Have you ever been too busy driving to take time to get gas?"[3]

If we have an assignment that's due in sixty minutes, we think, *I need to get to work.* We think more preparation is out of the question because we need every minute to find a solution. In reality, every minute we spend planning dramatically compresses the time needed to complete the task.

Preparation is the catalyst for all success. It's also the quickest path to confidence for introverts.

## The Confidence Factor

Introverts are deep thinkers. We don't just toss out an idea and see where it lands; we form it, explore it, then think through the options. The upside is that we have a unique ability to shape world-class ideas that have structure and depth. The downside is that we often have a tough time responding spontaneously when someone asks our opinion before we've thought it through.

When that happens and we're not sure what to say, we often feel like we've failed. When we review our performance later and think of all the things we could have said, we beat ourselves up for our inability to think quickly. We don't feel confident and we don't feel capable. We're not critiquing the issue anymore; we're evaluating our personal worth.

Sounds kind of extreme, right? Not if we've experienced it. It's easy to think we're the only ones with the problem since everyone else sounds so confident. But if we're analyzing the situation honestly, it wasn't everyone; it was a few people. We didn't notice the others who weren't saying anything either because . . . they weren't saying anything. If we're feeling a lack of confidence, others are too.

The same thing happens when we're given an assignment that's out of our comfort zone. If it's something we're not familiar with, it's easy to focus on all the things that could go wrong, how hard it will be, and how high the chance of failure is. It's painful, and it seems like there's no way around that pain. It seems logical to an extrovert that putting all that energy into preparation instead of worry would build confidence, but this might not be intuitive for an introvert. If there's an inner belief that says *I can't do this*, it's hard to see the potential of a simple solution.

Different temperaments look at the same situation in different ways.

This isn't a new problem. Two thousand years ago, Jesus told a story that's recorded in the Bible about the same situation. Look carefully at the situation, then consider how introverts and extroverts read the same story differently. Jesus said:

> Is there anyone here who, planning to build a new house, doesn't first sit down and figure the cost so you'll know if you can complete it? If you only get the foundation laid and then run out of money, you're going to look pretty foolish. Everyone passing by will poke fun at you: "He started something he couldn't finish." (Luke 14:28–30)

Most extroverts read that story and think, *Whoa—if I don't prepare, I won't get to finish the project and it'll get in the way of my success.* The focus is on their own performance. Most introverts read that story and think, *Whoa—if I don't prepare, everyone will poke fun at me.* The focus is on the reactions of others.

When it's been a pattern over a lifetime, it's easy for us to believe we'll never have the confidence we need to excel in the business world, and that we'll always be scrambling to hold our own in conversations.

It doesn't have to be that way. With a clear understanding and commitment to preparation, introverts can excel and shine in any situation.

Some people believe "preparation" means thinking of all the questions someone might ask, then memorizing responses to each one. In real life, it doesn't matter how many questions you've prepped for; the other person will always ask the one question you hadn't considered, and you're stuck without an answer.

Instead, we should think of preparation as looking into the subject from different angles in order to understand it, not to win a debate. For example, if you're going into a meeting where the results of an internal company survey will be presented and discussed, most people (introverts and extroverts alike) figure they'll wait until they're in the meeting to find out the details. For an introvert, that puts you at a disadvantage if you're called on for your thoughts, because it's all hitting you cold. You haven't had time to process.

Instead, see if you can get a copy of the survey results ahead of time and familiarize yourself with the content. It won't take long. You certainly won't be prepared to give a formal presentation on it, but if you're asked to share your opinion during the meeting, you won't be caught off guard. You'll feel confident in responding because you can relate what's being discussed to information you already know.

If you try to engage me in a discussion of driving habits in America versus Greenland, I'll be at a loss to know what to say. But if you ask me for the same comparison of American versus Ethiopian drivers, I'm all in. I've spent time in that country and have ridden in taxis and private cars there, and I know how it differs from similar experiences in the United States.

I'm not confident talking about driving in Greenland because I have no background there; I'm unprepared. I'm much more comfortable talking about Ethiopian driving because of my experience; I'm prepared for that conversation. But if I found out that our team would be discussing driving in Greenland, I could do some research ahead of the meeting to build my knowledge. I wouldn't be able to speak from experience, but I'd be able to draw from what I'd learned in my preparation.

The better prepared introverts are, the more confident we'll be in any situation.

## The Power of Preparation

There's something about preparation that makes us feel better. Research has shown that if we take the time to prepare in one specific area, our brains work to make us feel more confident in unrelated areas at the same time. Preparing gives us a better outlook, period.[4]

I spent over three decades teaching seminars in hundreds of companies, from mom-and-pop storefronts to Fortune 100 corporations. I led about a hundred sessions each year on various aspects of communication, leadership, and productivity. That meant that nearly every day I'd go into a new environment and culture. It was a major commitment for these companies to pull their people away from work for a day of growth, so it was important that the experience provided exactly the outcomes they were looking for.

As an introvert, I needed to do more than know the subject well and go through the presentation. I also needed to have as clear an understanding as possible of the specific needs of the audience and the expectations of the client. I wasn't there to perform a show; I was there to help them take their people to a new level of knowledge, engagement, and execution.

Early in my career, I would call the client to see what time I should arrive, where to park, how long the lunch break would be, and what the room setup would be like. My preparation was all about logistics, making sure I felt comfortable.

It didn't take long to realize this wasn't serving the client's needs. Soon, with the help of colleagues and my own company's standards, I learned what my preparation needed to look like before every seminar. That included a lengthy phone call (this was before virtual calls) to learn about the culture, the issues, and why they chose to invest in this experience. That call was a chance to build a relationship with my contact person and connect well before the session. My agenda for the call was to discover the unique challenges they faced and customize the experience to achieve those ends.

Did I learn everything about the company through those phone calls? Nope, and that's OK. But I prepared enough in gaining some understanding of their uniqueness that I felt confident tailoring the experience to their situation. I wasn't a vendor presenting a class; I was a partner helping them make a difference.

I still needed to know the logistics of the day. The more I knew about those details, the less stress I had driving there in the morning. In those early days (before the internet), I would study paper maps to find the best route. If I was teaching locally in the Los Angeles area, there was always the risk of something happening on the freeway that would get me stuck in standstill traffic. Knowing that, I often would leave my home at 4:30 or 5:00 in the morning so I could beat the traffic, then hang out at a coffee shop and get some work done. Typically, nothing would happen—but I'd rather get somewhere early and relax with a cup of coffee than be stuck in traffic wondering if I would get there on time (especially if I was teaching a class on time management).

## The Pattern of Preparation

Speaker Roger Crawford said, "The quality of your preparation will influence the quality of your performance."[5] That's true in just about every area of life. If you want to know what outcomes you're going to achieve (including what you do and how you feel), simply look at your level of preparation.

Pilots go through a thorough inspection of their plane before every flight. They use a printed checklist that covers every detail necessary for making sure everything is working before they start the engine. You'd think that if someone had been a pilot for decades they could skip that inspection, or at least not use the printed list. After all, they've done it so many times that it should be second nature by now, right?

Nope. They still use the list. They know that over time, familiarity could cause simple oversights that could bring the plane down, so they want to prepare for anything that could possibly happen. They don't just hope for the best; they prepare with precision so they can take off with confidence. (It also gives the passengers confidence to see the pilot's careful preparation.)

This is also a good way to approach every day. At the beginning of each day, think through all the opportunities you have on your schedule. Consider each one and ask yourself these three questions:

- *What will probably happen that I expect?*
- *What could go wrong that I don't expect?*
- *How can I best prepare for both?*

Consider working from an outcome list instead of a to-do list. Don't just look at your day as a bunch of activities. Think in terms of what needs to have happened by the end of the day—the outcomes. What can you do to prepare to keep less important activities from stealing your attention from mission-critical outcomes? The greater the risk and the more impactful the outcome, the more important it is to prepare well.

When your day gets crazy, preparation can interrupt that flow of craziness. Step back and catch your breath, then take time to evaluate what's happening. Otherwise, you'll find yourself in damage control instead of self-control, and the urgent things will keep you from doing the important things. Chaos steals perspective, which robs us of the ability to make the best decisions. Preparation doesn't have to take an hour—just a minute or two where you can step back and see the big picture again before jumping back into the battle.

Preparation and outcomes go together. The more intentionally you prepare, the better the outcomes. The less you prepare, the shakier the outcomes.

The best news? When preparation becomes the standard operating system for introverts, it helps us realize that success is not just possible but *probable*.

No, there's not a magic pill to help us succeed in everything. But if we can develop a bias toward preparation and make it part of our daily practice, both our confidence and the results will rise exponentially . . . almost like magic!

### Coming Up

We've explored all seven Master Moves that give a competitive advantage to introverts in the workplace:

1. Learning to speak extrovert.
2. Managing energy for peak performance.
3. Creating influence through gentle persuasion.
4. Building trust.
5. Nurturing emotional intelligence.
6. Customizing our work environment.
7. Ensuring success through intentional preparation.

Don't worry about getting them perfect from the start. All of these are things you can grow into, taking the tiniest steps possible. Over time, you'll begin to feel your confidence rising as you're better able to navigate an extroverted world.

The final stage in the journey is to figure out how to apply these to your own work environment and relationships.

It'll be worth the effort!

# PART 3

# THRIVING AT WORK

"OK, I get it," I hear you saying. "Being an introvert is a good thing, and I see that with the right mindset, I can capitalize on my unique strengths, feel good about myself, and make a difference. I see that I can celebrate who I am and my unique temperament.

"But my boss and coworkers haven't read the book. They think we should all work the same way. I can see my strengths, but my work culture doesn't always value those strengths. So, how do I make it work at work?"

That's the gap. Introverts can feel better about ourselves and our unique qualities, but we still have to go to work in environments where we may be expected to perform by extrovert standards and expectations:

- We're expected to speak up in meetings before we've had a chance to process our thoughts.
- We're put on teams where it's tough to navigate strong personalities that take over and ignore our ideas.
- We're overlooked for promotion because we don't demonstrate traditional leadership skills.

- We end up in management positions with teams who simply won't let us lead.
- We feel like nobody understands us or values our ideas (or even gives us a chance to express those ideas).
- We're often intimidated when talking to executives and people above us.

That's what this final section is about. Earlier we mentioned how there are a lot of great books dealing with introversion, including some great resources to help extroverted leaders catch the vision of designing an introvert-friendly workplace. Other books build on research studies to clarify what introverts need and celebrate our uniqueness. Now, what we need isn't theory; it's a simple, practical set of tools and approaches that help us succeed.

This book stands alone in answering one simple question: *How can I thrive as an introvert in a work environment?*

The seven Master Moves we learned in part 2 enable us to excel in every life situation. They're skills anyone could use but that introverts will find can become second nature.

With those Master Moves as the foundation, let's focus on the workplace. We all realize that the chance of getting our work culture to change is about the same as beauty pageant contestants achieving world peace. But there are six critical work situations that apply to every employee, no matter what their temperament:

- Crafting your career.
- Working well with others.
- Becoming visible.
- Leading your people.
- Communicating with confidence.
- Focusing on a greater purpose.

Introverts can find these situations challenging because we assume they require extrovert skills. However, with the right mindset, understanding, and skill in the Master Moves, we can use our uniqueness to become highly successful in any of these situations.

Let's get practical as we explore the landscape.

13

# Crafting Your Career

Don't pick a job with great vacation time. Pick a career that
doesn't need escaping from.

Unknown

Remember how you felt when you applied for your first job?
For most people, it was a blend of equal parts fear and excitement. Excitement, because you felt like you were sticking
your toes into the shallow end of adulthood. Fear, because you
really didn't know what it was going to be like. And when you
got that first yes, you experienced a sense of validation. You had
something to offer and somebody noticed—and was willing to
pay you to do it.

A first interview can be challenging because we're not
sure what kind of person they're looking for. If we took
any classes that talked about the interview process, we were
told to make good eye contact and smile, have some questions of our own ready, and be friendly, warm, and outgoing.

"You're competing against a lot of other candidates," we're told. "So, make sure you're positive and upbeat during the conversation."

In other words, we might feel like we're supposed to act like an extrovert.

The problem word here is *act*. We're tempted to act in a certain way to match what we think an interviewer is looking for. If we're applying for a job as a manager, we act like what we think a manager should act like. If we're interviewing for a sales position, we try to match the common image of a salesperson. We're trying to convince them that we have what it takes to do the job.

An interview is supposed to help the interviewer know what you're really like. If you act like someone you're not, you're misrepresenting yourself. You might get hired, but you could lose the job once they figure out you're not who they thought you were.

This goes both ways. You might find out that the expectations of the job are different from what was presented during the interview. You can find yourself disillusioned. After a while, you'll realize you have a choice: you can leave, or you can try to make it work.

Throughout your career, you'll always have that balancing act. There are good parts and bad parts to every job. That's true for everyone, no matter what their temperament. The challenge is deciding what you can live with.

For introverts, there are specific challenges that come with a new position. Maybe your workplace doesn't recognize the unique contributions of introverts, so they expect everyone to function like extroverts:

- Meetings are filled with free-flowing discussions, and there's an expectation of frequent and spontaneous contribution.

- Deep thinking and contemplation aren't necessarily valued, since it takes time away from getting the job done.
- Well-meaning bosses often feel like it's their job to help their introverted employees become more engaged and outgoing so they can demonstrate their ability to contribute.

It's true all the way up the corporate ladder, and it will be true throughout your career. One study showed that highly extroverted people are 25 percent more likely to secure top executive positions (since they're chosen for their extroverted skills), but introverts consistently make the most effective leaders because of their unique thinking abilities, emotional intelligence, insights, and ideas.[1]

The best way to start and manage your career is with honesty. Be totally honest with yourself and others about who you are and capitalize on your unique strengths. Never try to pretend you're something you're not; it's too much work and it sets you up for a career-long pattern of maintaining an image.

## Hidden Strengths

My fourth-grade teacher asked us to select a book from the school library to read and prepare an oral report. A couple of weeks later, we would present our reports to the class. Normally, being called up to the front of the class wouldn't be an introvert's first choice. But I wasn't worried, because I had plenty of time to prepare. (I didn't know at the time that preparation was a Master Move that would give me confidence, but I must have just sensed it.)

However, one skill I hadn't learned yet as a nine-year-old was overcoming procrastination. I knew I had several weeks to read and prepare, so each day I put it off until the next day.

Eventually, I forgot about the assignment. The book was in my desk at school, out of sight and off my radar.

Until one Monday morning.

Ms. Domini announced, "Today, we'll get to hear your oral book reports. We'll go in alphabetical order by last name, and you'll have three minutes each." I knew I had two options: stand up and admit that I hadn't done the assignment, or fake it. The first option was unthinkable, so I took the risk of the second option. I quickly thought through the last names in the room and realized I would be the third speaker. That would give me six minutes to figure out what to say and overcome my terror.

The book had a paper jacket, and the front and back flaps gave a description of the content and storyline without revealing the ending. I quickly read through the summary and mentally captured the major points, then made up a couple of applications of how the content would be helpful.

I walked to the front of the room and started with "Have you ever," and laid out the context of the story. I introduced the main character and set the stage for the drama. I basically read the book jacket description, trying not to look at it too often. At the end I said, "How does it end? Well, obviously I'm not going to spoil it for you. But I did learn a couple of things that I really found helpful."

It took a couple of days to get through all of the reports. When we were done, Ms. Domini said, "You all did great work. If I were to pick one report as the 'winner,' it would be Mike's. It really shows how well we can do things when we take the time to prepare."

It wasn't my greatest moment of integrity and honesty. Hopefully, I've grown in those areas since that episode. Yes, I was an introvert (though I didn't know what that was at the time) and was always terrified if I was called on to contribute something spontaneously in front of others. But I learned that if I had advance notice and a chance to prepare—even if it was only six minutes—I was always comfortable in front of a group. It was a unique part of my wiring.

Decades later, that hasn't changed. I will always panic when I'm called on in a group setting. But give me a few minutes to think first, and I'm good to go.

We're all gifted in different ways. When you've been in uncomfortable situations as an introvert, you've developed ways of responding so others don't see your struggle. You might call them "coping mechanisms" because you've used them for so long, and it feels like you're "cheating." You think you don't have the conversational skills an extrovert does, so your way of handling those situations feels like an attempt to survive. But if you look closer, you might find that these ways of responding are your gifts of communication—and you're not valuing them sufficiently.

When a conversation gets uncomfortable, maybe you've learned how to change the subject without the other person realizing what happened. You feel that if you were a "legitimate" conversationalist, you'd stay in the dialogue and hold your own as you talked. But that's using an extrovert standard to critique your natural ability to impact the direction a conversation is taking. That ability to guide the direction of a conversation in the moment is a powerful tool that focuses more on process than content, which is an area of strength for an introvert.

Maybe your company started a new initiative, and you're uncomfortable with what it could mean for your daily responsibilities. It looks like you're going to have to take on tasks and projects that are out of your skillset. What can you do? You can identify and preemptively volunteer to take on a role that best fits your natural strengths. Outline the value you could bring by coordinating some of the behind-the-scenes work or organizing the structure of the new project. Maybe you can be the point person for keeping the project on track and making sure everyone presents their results in a timely manner.

If you find yourself feeling like that's avoiding the "real work," remember that you're personalizing the initiative so you can work in your sweet spot, bringing value no one else can bring the way you can.

By exploring the ways you can adapt creatively in different situations, you can create opportunities to thrive using your natural gifts. Be honest with yourself about what you're good at and what you're not, then hone your strengths into tools that can make a genuine contribution in your workplace.

## Give Up the Excuses

Never let your introversion keep you from reaching your full potential. Become keenly aware of your strengths and find ways to use them as a foundation for your career. They should be your launchpad, not your landing pad—use them in proactively pursuing amazing opportunities that could be highly engaging and professionally rewarding.

Make a commitment to understand your strengths and use them well. Others might get more natural notice, but you're good at observing—so you'll ask the deeper and more relevant questions that can steer an entire discussion in a creative direction or help people see a new perspective. Develop the new skills needed to present your ideas clearly, such as building an easy-to-follow structure, being concise, and adding interesting, relevant examples of your points. When you learn these skills for communicating clearly, you increase your ability to contribute. You offer your colleagues your valuable perspective because you express it well.

Don't try to learn all the skills you need at once. Anytime you try to move out of your comfort zone, it's going to be uncomfortable. If you move too far, too fast, it can feel like you're in the middle of a desert during summer with no food, no water, and no cell signal. If you take tiny steps of growth,

154

your comfort zone is still nearby. Build your skills slowly and solidly in the context of what's familiar, and each new skill will expand your comfort zone.

For example, maybe it's way out of your comfort zone to speak up in meetings. If it's a regularly scheduled meeting, see if you can get a copy of the agenda ahead of time or ask about the topics that will be covered. Then take the time to think through each item and come up with a single, thought-provoking question for each item that others probably won't bring up.

During the meeting, look for an opportunity to jump in with at least one question for the group. You don't have to have answers, just pose the question for others to consider. If it's tough to get a word in edgewise, raise your hand to catch someone's attention. In a virtual call, someone will notice and say, "Becky—looks like you have something to add?" That's your opening to ask your question: "You know, I think there's one thing we might want to consider. How do you think our clients will feel about this change?"

That's it. People will notice your contribution. Do it often, and it will get easier—and you'll build a reputation for the valuable perspectives you offer to the group.

No matter where you are in your career, always have one area in which you've made a commitment to grow. Invest in yourself slowly, and the compound effect will give you powerful ways to make an impact.

## Working for the Long Haul

Over the years, I've met thousands of employees in companies where I've been presenting workshops. I often ask someone, "How long have you worked here?" Often, the answer has been thirty or forty years. I usually say, "Wow—that's amazing! You must really like what you do to stick around that long."

Sometimes they agree, but often they say, "No, the work is just a job. But the retirement benefits are good, and that's what I'm working for." They often know exactly how many days they have left before they retire, even if it's a decade or more away.

I don't hear that as much anymore, since pension plans aren't the norm. But I've often thought about how many people don't enjoy their work. It's a way to make a living, and it's comfortable, so they just do it to get to the end.

That might be true for you if you haven't discovered ways to customize your work environment so you can cultivate your unique skills. When you recognize what's possible by being totally yourself, you'll be energized by your ability to create exponential value through your contributions.

Learning to be the best "you" possible enables you to build a long-term career that makes you want to get up and go to work every morning. That's why you want to pick a career for the energy it gives you, not just for the money. Identify your unique strengths and weaknesses, then hold them up to any job description you're considering to see if it's a fit. If you're further along in your career, evaluate your current job (or potential new job) the same way and see if it is challenging enough for your current level of passion and expertise.

We've all heard the phrase, "Bloom where you're planted." That doesn't mean you can never change careers or employers; it means that investing in yourself can make the difference in how "good" a job is. If a garden isn't blooming, it's usually easier to fertilize what's already planted than to replace all the plants.

No matter where you are in your career, focus on those little areas of growth that can make your career meaningful. Consider these practical options:

- Be intentional about building your schedule before each week begins. If others have access to your calendar, make sure you've blocked off plenty of time for recharging, preparation, and just getting work done. If you don't get to your schedule first, you're leaving it open to the priorities of others.

- Know and utilize your unique strengths and avoid comparisons with the strengths of others. Be totally yourself. Somebody else might be good at making phone calls, but you might craft killer emails and design simple, persuasive presentation decks.
- Realize that rest isn't optional and work it into your life. Anytime you have a big presentation, team meeting, or conference, schedule downtime before and after as appropriate. If your colleagues all go out after the day's activities, be willing to say no without apology: "Love you guys, but I need some downtime."
- Decide what environments energize you and get in those environments often. It might be a quiet room in your house, a local beach or park early in the morning, or a short break in your car during lunch.
- Analyze your social needs and structure around them. If you're meeting someone for coffee, tell them what time you'll need to leave (and stick to it). If attending a social event, remember that you don't have to socialize with everyone in the room. If you get to spend some quality time with one or two people, the event has been a success for you.
- Get creative with your strengths. Listen to the discussion in meetings, take notes, problem solve in your head, then send a summary email with a fully-thought-out solution to stakeholders after the meeting. You're making a meaningful contribution from your unique skills.

If you want to thrive throughout your career, be yourself! Learn what your real strengths are, embrace them, and find creative ways to implement them. Never compare with anyone else, because they're not you. Never pretend in order to impress others. The more you can be you, the more impressed others will be.

It's a blend of character and competence. If you learn to be completely yourself, you can thrive in any environment while being true to yourself . . . throughout your entire career.

## 14

# Working Well with Others

Sometimes you meet someone and you know from the first moment that you want to spend your whole life without them.

Unknown

Getting a new job can feel like moving to another country. You're in a new environment surrounded by people you don't know. It's a different culture. You might not speak the same language. They all know each other, and you feel like an intruder. They know how to do the job in that environment, and you're just starting. They know where to find the bathroom and the copy machine and who to ask for the things they need.

It's uncomfortable. You're the new person, and you believe everyone is sizing you up—and you're doing the same with them. You pretend you're OK and try to show how excited you are to be part of this team. You know from past experience that you'll figure it out, but the learning curve feels high. And if you're remote, you have to do all of that through technology instead of in person.

You might have the urge to get back in your jammies and curl up on the couch with a bag of cheese puffs, but that feeling will pass when you start taking action. Moving forward is a simple choice when you realize that *somebody's paying you to figure it out and make it work*.

The reality is that now you're part of a new team. These people don't have to become your best friends, but you'll start thriving when you figure out how to work with them. Focus on your common ground: you're all there to do what the boss wants and help the company move forward.

No company offers someone a job and says, "We know you need money, so just show up and we'll give it to you." They hire you because they believe you can help the company succeed. They're placing a bet on you—that you'll perform in a way that gives them a greater return on their investment than the amount of money they're paying you.

That should be encouraging and energizing, because you passed the first test—the interview. Somebody has affirmed that you have what it takes. You've been "launched" in this new adventure, and now you can put your knowledge, experience, and skills in play. You get to make a difference, and the organization will become stronger because you're part of it.

## First Approach

New people are often told, "We're family here." Don't believe it—they're not, and they shouldn't be. A work team is not a group of siblings who are free to squabble, leave a mess, and make bodily noises. These are coworkers who need to cooperate and collaborate toward a common end, which means you do different things than you'd do with family. However, you'll spend a lot of time with these people, so you want to build appropriate relationships that make the work process a smooth, enjoyable experience.

They don't know you, and you don't know them. What are appropriate ways to begin connecting with your new colleagues?

We've all seen new people go out of their way to impress colleagues, trying to demonstrate how competent and friendly and collaborative they are. As a new addition to an existing group, they'll suggest new and different ways of doing things to streamline processes or work in a more efficient way together. They're trying to prove their value—but this approach often backfires.

Instead of being impressed, the existing group members may think, *Who do you think you are to come in and change the way we do things? You don't even know us, and you're telling us that our way isn't good enough.* In so many words, they're saying, "You're not one of us."

Rather than trying to impress your new teammates, a better approach is to look for ways to win their trust. A simple alternative would be to ask questions of the existing team members about how they do their job. Join in and learn from them. "You've been at this for a long time," you could ask. "How have you made the process work?" You're acknowledging their expertise, and it helps you connect with the group, because you're not trying to impress them.

Once you've learned the job process well and performed it as part of the team for a while, you might suggest one simple tweak that might simplify a process for everyone. Since you've built trust, your input will be received differently because you're seen as one of the group.

This approach comes naturally for an introvert. You're being yourself, not pretending. You're there to serve the people around you, not to convince them to like you. Make it your goal to help others become better and stronger because they have your support.

Some of your coworkers will be extroverts, some will be introverts. You can build relationships with both by seeing them as individuals and getting to know them one-on-one. That implements the Master Moves of *building trust* and *emotional intelligence*—building personal relationships with each person uniquely instead of with the group as a whole.

Lead with your competence and character. Competence shows that you have what it takes to do the job well, which builds your credibility. Character is shown in your desire to build trust, which comes when you have a mindset of serving others.

## Connecting with Extroverts

Once you've built trust, explore ways to work together more effectively to make introversion a natural part of the conversation.

Let's say you want to build a relationship with one of the extroverts on your team. Find some one-on-one time with them. Then ask questions to explore their background, their interests, and how they work best in the company. Find out what their unique needs are and explore what makes them successful. Let them know you value that information because you want to do everything you can to support them.

They might say they get impatient when someone gives too much detail when describing what they want or when trying to build a case for something. "I don't want all the background," they say. "I just need them to spit it out and tell me what they need. Then I can ask questions."

Your response could be, "That's so helpful. I work differently, and my tendency is to focus on a lot of details. So, when I come to you about something, I should figure out my main points and keep it concise so you get the basic idea, then give you greater detail when you ask questions. Is that kind of what you're saying?"

That dialogue can open the door for you to share briefly about how you work best, since they've just told you what works best for them. "When I'm in a meeting or a conversation, it takes me longer to process what people say. I don't share my ideas until that's happened. So, I won't talk as much in meetings, but I can come back later with some carefully crafted solutions and ideas. I also work best when people don't put me on the spot, but I can bring a whole different perspective or ask the questions nobody else is thinking about."

The next time you're in a meeting, you can bet that extrovert won't be spontaneously calling on you for your ideas in the moment. But they also won't overlook you just because you're not initiating much. They'll know you've got something valuable to offer and might even mention that you'll have some good things to share once you've thought it through. They might even call on you and simply ask, "I know you think about these things from a careful perspective. Does it feel like we're missing anything, or do you see any red flags about what we've been saying?"

This approach isn't manipulative. It's an honest way for an introvert to simply get to know others by exploring each person's uniqueness, earning the right to share your own unique way of working as well.

## What about the Boss?

Character and competence are also key to winning the respect of your manager. In most cases, you probably won't begin by asking them out to lunch or connecting in the same way you would with your peers and colleagues. They hired you, and now they're watching to see if they made a good choice.

What does that look like? You've figured out how to perform the job well that they hired you for, and you're a positive force on the team. If you can take initiative and go beyond their expectations in a few areas, it will set you apart in the group. Because of your performance, you've built trust. You can use that as a way to talk about your unique needs if it comes up.

When you have one-on-ones or performance reviews, your manager might make suggestions about "being more engaged in meetings" or "contributing more ideas to the group." That's an indication they have an extrovert mindset, so this is a chance to help them understand the unique contribution you're able to make in the context of their expectations. Listen carefully to what they suggest and let them know you're willing to build more skills in the areas they've suggested. Don't lecture them on the unique needs of an introvert, but use your sensitive approach to show how genuine engagement might look different for you—with practical ideas and alternatives.

The first Master Move we learned was how to *speak extrovert*. This could be a natural opportunity to coach your extroverted manager to learn the language of an introvert as well. Discuss some of the words and speech patterns used by extroverts that you've learned, asking for your manager's perspective. You might add examples of how an introvert would say the same things differently. You may help your manager become bilingual too!

Let your manager know that tossing ideas out during a meeting isn't your strongest play. Listening to the ideas that are shared and processing them to build creative perspectives and solutions is where you can contribute most effectively. Share that you're especially good at seeing what's being overlooked during a discussion—so maybe you could work toward their suggestion of "being more engaged" by asking key questions instead of sharing new ideas. Suggest that the manager allow you to be mostly quiet during those meetings, but then call on you near the end with the same questions mentioned earlier: "Are we missing anything? Is there anything we're not thinking of?"

That's how you can prove your worth to your manager—reminding them that the introverts in the group have a wealth of knowledge and perspective that can enrich everyone and bring a whole new level of creativity and depth to any discussion.

When issues come up that need the attention of a manager, never just complain. Use your skills of observation and analysis to craft a clear picture of what's happening and the negative impact it's having on productivity, morale, or other issues. Then offer possible solutions, including what it would take to implement them. They might not use all of your solutions, but you've been proactive with your approach to helping them with a well-thought-out understanding of the issue. If it's appropriate, offer to take the lead in implementing the solution—or working with them to craft a new direction.

That's what it means for an employee to add value. Your manager took the risk and hired you, hoping your contribution would provide an exponential return on their investment. Most people try to do their job well. An introvert has a deeper well to draw from to add value that others might not know exists. When you create a carefully crafted solution, you'll be building a reputation for adding unique value.

## Simple Steps

Relationship building is not rocket science; it's genuinely caring about others instead of getting them to care about you. Most of the things you can do are just common sense, but common sense isn't necessarily common practice.

Here are comfortable ways to build relationships with other people:

*Don't pretend to be someone you're not.* Be you.
*Take the initiative and be the first to reach out.* Introverts often avoid initiating conversations because we're not

sure how the other person will respond. Many people feel the same way and are waiting for someone to break the ice. If you're the first to say hello, you've set the relationship in motion.

*Ask open-ended questions.* People like to talk about themselves and respond well to genuine interest. It's natural for them to follow up by asking you the same questions, so think through your answers ahead of time.

*Follow them on social media.* Comment in person about something they posted that caught your attention (puppy pictures, not political views).

*Make eye contact.* That's usually not hard for an introvert, and it's the quickest way to a real connection. Someone called eye contact an "emotional handshake." (Since the pandemic, that might be an emotional fist bump.)

*Ask for help.* Anytime you ask for advice or assistance, you're acknowledging their expertise and respecting their opinion. Keep it simple, but you've affirmed the other person.

*Smile.* A smile makes you more approachable. It doesn't have to be a big, artificial smile; just let your face show that you're glad you encountered someone, no matter who it is.

*Work on your posture.* It sounds trite, but good posture exudes confidence. Confidence makes people want to connect with you. Don't use it as a gimmick; work on your confidence first, then make sure the way you carry yourself simply demonstrates it.

*Attend social events, but redefine your objective.* When you have to attend a meeting or conference, you don't have to connect with everyone in the room. Make it your goal to have two or three healthy conversations. Have one with someone you already know, and then reach out to at least one person you haven't met. Look for common ground and explore it at a comfortable length instead of making small talk with everyone in the room. Then leave early so you can recharge.

## Make It Real

If you want to build relationships at work, become a "social introvert." That means you get to keep all of your unique strengths and characteristics and operate in your most comfortable zone by being fully yourself. At the same time, it's not that hard to learn to make simple steps of connection. Just add a little bit of connection during each day—something as simple as taking a quick break, dropping into someone's cubicle, and saying, "Just on a quick break. You good?" See what they say, then follow up and ask them about it the next day.

There's an old introvert paradigm that says it's dishonest to fake interest in people just to get ahead at work. Change the paradigm by taking simple steps to grow into the relationship-building skills we've discussed, and you're being completely honest.

You're becoming the best "you" you can possibly be!

## 15

# Becoming Visible

The only thing worse than being talked about is not being talked about.

Oscar Wilde

nvisible" is an introvert's favorite color.

Every introvert is different, so it's tough to make assumptions that apply to everyone. But in general, we tend to move toward the back while extroverts move toward the front. We pick seats along the edges while extroverts head for the middle. We look forward to staying in while extroverts look forward to going out. We prefer keeping things in our heads while extroverts prefer to let them out.

It takes effort to do things out of our default settings. Introverts aren't usually comfortable with self-promotion, so it takes an intentional choice for us to overcome inertia and be seen. Extroverts find it easy to be outgoing and visible, and it takes an intentional choice if they recognize a need to step back and let others take the spotlight.

Introverts often slide into the background—possibly doing stellar work and making huge creative and strategic contributions, but we're not on anyone's radar. People might recognize us, but we're not "top of mind."

To be successful at work, you want to make a difference. When you're visible, you have an advantage. When you're not visible, you have a great disadvantage. You might do your job well, but people won't notice if you're doing it in the shadows. How can introverts become seen, known, and heard without pretending to be extroverts?

## Overcoming Inertia

I was twelve when I contracted mononucleosis and had to stay home from school for six weeks. My parents would pick up my homework from the teacher a couple of times a week and bring it home for me to complete. It was the best six weeks of school I never had. I could work at my own pace without distraction, and I probably learned more during that time than in any classroom experience I'd had up to that point. I was doing good work, but I was off everybody's radar. I'll have to admit it was challenging when I went back to school and wasn't alone anymore.

Being alone like that might feel good, and it might work for a season—and it's something we settle into easily. Unfortunately, that's not the way things work in business. It's OK to be 100 percent introverted but not OK to work in a solitary way 100 percent of the time. Even introverts need other people, especially if we want to be seen.

Working remotely poses a challenge for us. It seems ideal, because we can simply do the work without the same level of social interaction. But after a while, it's easy to get used to working alone and become too introspective and lose energy. We can settle into our comfortable introversion and get stuck in our quiet lifestyle. Every introvert needs a certain level of interaction to stay energized and connected.

It's a matter of finding the right balance. Too much isolation is tough to overcome, and going back to an office requires an intentional effort to vanquish inertia. It starts with a mindset shift that moves from *I have to work with others* to *I get to work with others*. It means recognizing the value of working in a low-stimulation environment while appreciating the value of connection—both personally and professionally.

One recent study surveyed therapists for suggestions for making that transition to in-person work successfully:

- Ask questions and plan ahead, which calms the brain.
- Visit the office ahead of time to explore changes, such as your desk being in a new place or new technology being used.
- Don't minimize what might seem like childish concerns. If you never wear shoes at home, ask permission to do the same at the office. If you miss your pet, get a home camera to check in on them.
- Grieve the loss of your home routine, then focus on what you're gaining by returning to the office. List the advantages and pursue them as opportunities to stretch and grow.[1]

It's important to check your self-talk. Interacting with others can feel like a whole lot of work. It can seem like everyone else has never-ending energy and can't get enough of interacting with each other, and you're the only one who needs a break to recharge. Keep in mind that your goal is to interact with others in a way that showcases your work *and* works for you too.

Make sure you're getting your own tank refilled by crafting alone time into your schedule. At the same time, make sure you also have time to fill the tanks of others by investing in a few key relationships. Otherwise, you risk becoming like the Dead Sea. Water flows into it but never flows out—so it becomes a place where nothing can live.

## The Process of Presence

Let's say you're part of a team that meets regularly. Whether it's in person or virtually, each person tends to engage in a way that's most comfortable for them. Their individual temperaments will determine the working dynamic of the group—which usually means extroverts take the lead, while introverts have to be more intentional to be heard.

One way to change this is to choose to stretch out of your comfort zone and do something different. That's an advantage for an introvert, because you can utilize your Master Moves to influence the way the group works together:

- Communicate in your own way. It's your superpower.
- Anytime you can't think of anything to say, ask a question. You're both contributing and steering.
- Keep your contributions simple. Build a reputation for saying a lot in a few words.
- Don't fear extroverts; build partnerships with them.
- Don't assume that extroverts are trying to shut you down with their comments. They're sharing and probably aren't even thinking about you.
- Connect with other team members one-on-one to build real relationships. Explore both of your accomplishments and experience that might not come out in a group meeting.

- Do stellar work. Make sure others know what you did by sharing without bragging.

In other words, be fully present. When you're working on a team, don't just focus on the mechanics of the task. Focus on the uniqueness of each person, acknowledge it, and tap into it. We are especially adept at recognizing this, and it can move us to a whole new level of influence within the group.

It's common for introverts to share from our expertise but not from our daily life. Doing so might feel less vulnerable but robs you of the best tool you have to build real relationships. Let others get to know you and your life outside of the cubicle.

Always work from your strengths, not from the expectations you think others have of you. Becoming visible isn't a performance; it's a process of being yourself and capitalizing on your unique abilities. We tend to focus on the skills we don't have and wish we did. Instead, focus on the skills you do have. You always have the most power when you're using your strengths.

For example, introverts are often most effective when we can put our thoughts in writing instead of trying to express them verbally. There's a place for both methods, but learn to make the most of well-timed emails, appropriate texts, and written expressions of your thoughts. If you have a company newsletter or blog, volunteer to write an article for the next issue. It's a simple way to use a gift that instantly gives you visibility, even beyond your own team.

For a number of years, I presented seminars for a single division of a huge pharmaceutical corporation. Most of the people in that division got to know me over time as they attended different sessions I would facilitate. I asked the head of that division if they had a company-wide newsletter, and if so, if I could get the name of its editor. I reached out with a proposal to do a short monthly column, covering some aspect of practical productivity in the workplace. The editor agreed, and I wrote that column for several years. As a result, I gained exposure throughout the entire corporation and was repeatedly asked to speak at different events and bring seminars to other divisions as well.

It was a comfortable way to work within my strengths and dramatically increase my visibility within that company. I became their go-to subject matter expert by writing about four paragraphs each month, which usually took about fifteen minutes.

Never underestimate the value of working in your strengths. Always look for creative approaches to find visibility without just talking more.

## Virtual Visibility

Everything we've been discussing applies in a virtual environment as well. If you're working either part- or full-time from a home office, you'll discover the built-in challenges. Besides the normal dynamics of finding your voice in meetings, there are the uncomfortable additions of being on a screen with others. It often feels like there are certain people who lead the discussion, speaking over each other, while others languish in silence because they can't figure out how to get a word in edgewise.

Virtual visibility doesn't happen just because people can see you on the screen. It takes more intentionality than an in-person meeting, but it's not difficult. It just requires a little stretching to "show up."

I'd always been the listener and observer on most virtual calls, operating in my sweet spot. This allowed me to process without talking, but it also kept me in the background. I realized that people who talk in virtual meetings are seen as more competent and have more influence, so I knew I needed to contribute. Here's what helped me the most:

*I changed my mindset.* Usually when I thought of bringing something up, it felt like I was doing it to change how others perceived me. I wondered how they would respond if I said something in the meeting. *What will they think of me? Is this worth bringing up? What if I mess up?* It was all about me. So I worked on speaking up in order to contribute something of value, not just to be seen. That simple mindset change gave me a legitimate reason to say something that others would need and remember.

*I went for quality of words, not quantity.* I discovered that I didn't need to be constantly contributing throughout the meeting to become visible. If I simply stayed mentally engaged in the conversation, I could always think of a clarifying question to ask or perspective to suggest. If I spoke once in each meeting, it put me on people's radar.

*I asked for the agenda* (as mentioned earlier). There might not be one in writing, but I would at least reach out to the leader to see if I could get an idea of what we'd be covering. That way I could think through the issues ahead of time so I could focus on at least one area where I might be able to add value.

*I wrote comments in the chat section.* Sometimes I might have something to say but felt awkward just speaking up in a large virtual group. I found that if I added a concise thought in the chat, there would be a good chance the leader would pick up on it and ask me to comment verbally. I could then add a brief clarification that I was prepared for. (I also learned not to comment on other people's comments, such as writing "Great idea" or "I agree." Anything I wrote needed to add value to the discussion.)

*I went first.* I often had a good idea to share but was waiting for the right opportunity to mention it. Either that time never came, or someone else shared the same idea first. I learned that if I contributed early, it would establish me as an active participant—even if it was the only thing I shared. Often people would refer to my comment since it was one of the first things they heard in the meeting.

*I would ask a question.* It's easier to ask a thought-provoking question than to come up with new ideas. "We've been talking about (item) . . . what if we thought about it from this perspective?" Questions carry an expectation of further discussion. Comments can simply be ignored.

*I would mention the elephant in the room.* I learned that if I was concerned about the direction the discussion was going, there were always others feeling the same way. When I carefully brought it up, it would open the door for the others to add their perspective.

With the right perspective, virtual meetings can become a great platform for introverts without having to change who we are.

## Is Networking Necessary?

*Do I have to network? I sure hope not.* When we think of networking, most of us picture ourselves swimming in a pond filled with piranha. The chance of getting eaten alive is high, so why would we want to do it?

However, if we redefine *networking*, we can see it as a valuable way to increase our personal satisfaction and visibility in our career and work environments. The purpose of networking isn't to meet a bunch of people we don't know so we can all impress each other and trade business cards; it's to meet the right people in the right way that can help us serve others, share resources, and build relationships where we might partner in the future. There's no value in collecting business cards, but there's great value in expanding our circle of influence.

Networking often takes place in a formal event where the goal is to meet as many people as possible. Most introverts wouldn't attend that kind of event because it's crafted around the specific skills of an extrovert. If we're invited, our first thought is, *Why in the world would I want to do that?*

More often, we'll find ourselves networking at a large conference or meeting that has main sessions and breakout sessions interspersed with breaks to "mingle." If there are three hundred people in the room, it can feel completely overwhelming. The same can be true of a simple social event with a lot of people attending. We might want to make ourselves more visible, so we attend—but we can't wait until it's over.

Check out some of these ideas that can make networking more worthwhile and fit an introvert's temperament:

- Don't try to meet as many people as possible; just decide ahead of time who you'd like to meet. Focus on a few of the right people who can enhance your career (and you can enhance theirs).
- For introverts, networking feels contrived and awkward. Instead, think of networking as a powerful way to find your voice—where your unique creativity lets you find ways to gain a few meaningful connections that have immediate value.

- Arrive early to these events. There are fewer people there early, so you're not walking into a crowd. It's also easier to find the first person you want to connect with. Find out what you have in common (which might be your feelings about the event) and use it to explore perspectives.

- Keep in mind the things you've learned about the first person you connect with. When you're talking to someone else who shares something in common with them, make an introduction. You'll be acting as an informal host as you make it easier for both of them, since they don't have to make the effort to meet.

- Most of your connections will come from showing interest in another person. At the same time, it's natural to share your own perspectives and experiences. If that doesn't happen, it becomes a one-sided exchange. Don't try to inject your own accomplishments into the conversation but be ready to state them clearly if it comes up as a natural part of the dialogue. Hiding your strengths is dishonest, in the same way that "over-tooting" your own horn can come across as arrogant. Just be two real people sharing a few moments of real life.

- Reach out to people who aren't part of your work group. Sociologist Ronald Burt talks about "idea ruts," where groups tend to think in the same ways if they don't have outside input. He writes that people whose networks expand into other groups "are at higher risk of having good ideas."[2]

## Step into the Light

It might feel unnerving to take steps to be seen when it's easier to stay unseen. But when it comes to your career, being seen is a requirement for growth and advancement. If you're feeling like you're in a dead-end job with no hope for anything changing, that's a good sign it's time to step up.

The good news is that it won't be unnerving if the steps you take are (1) small enough and (2) within the bounds of your temperament. Introverts have every right to feel uncomfortable about a process that doesn't engage our native strengths and skills. If we follow our own path, there's genuine hope for excitement, growth, and adventure.

Fears are like cockroaches. They thrive when they're unseen in the dark, but turning on the light drives them away.

Time to take the first step into the light?

## 16

# Leading Your People

Leaders who don't listen will eventually be surrounded by people who have nothing to say.

Anonymous

One hundred years ago, leadership in the workplace looked different than it does today. Most people worked on a factory floor, and the boss had a "corner office"—a platform where he (it was always a man) sat and looked down on the entire operation. There was a prescribed way things were supposed to be done, and his job was to make sure everything met those standards. If something didn't, he would send down one of his managers to yell at the person doing it wrong. People could get fired for the smallest mistake and didn't have any recourse.

That really wasn't leading; it was *directing*. When you lead, there are people who follow you—and you're the one going first. When you direct, you stand behind others and tell them what to do.

As the story goes, President Dwight D. Eisenhower was once asked in the Oval Office about his philosophy of leadership. He found a piece of string on his desk, then asked his guest to push it forward. His guest couldn't do it because the string kept trailing behind where he was holding it. Eisenhower said, "Pull the string, and it will follow you wherever you wish. Push it, and it will go nowhere at all."[1]

Today, we understand that true leadership motivates people to do things because they want to do them, not because they're forced. It's a process that inspires people to take action, and the leader becomes someone others want to follow.

But why? And how? What kind of person attracts followers? Can an introvert be a leader?

## The Substance of a Leader

We've come a long way from those early days and have a much clearer picture of what leadership should be. We know that effective leadership inspires people to catch a vision of what's possible, for both the company and themselves—and then be motivated to act on that vision.

There's still a stereotype that an effective leader is all about personality and charisma. That often leads us to believe that we can't be good leaders because we're not noisy or forceful or decisive enough. We think of leaders who were great motivators, like Martin Luther King Jr., Winston Churchill, and Eleanor Roosevelt, and assume it was their outgoing personalities that uniquely equipped them for leadership—but all three of these people were introverts.

In reality, the quietest person in the room has the potential to be the most effective leader. That's the conclusion of Jim Collins, author of *Good to Great*, in his research. He studied hundreds of successful companies that were known for their world-class leaders and innovators. His conclusion? That personal charisma is largely irrelevant in successful leadership—and can even be dangerous.[2] He suggests that "leadership is not personality," and says that many of the best leaders he studied in various companies have what he calls a "charisma bypass."[3]

Extroverts can absolutely be powerful leaders, but so can introverts. Examples of introverts able to motivate others to think and act differently include some famous names we've already mentioned, such as Albert Einstein and Abraham Lincoln, but also include Meryl Streep, Sir Isaac Newton, Mark Zuckerberg, Marissa Mayer, Al Gore, Michael Jordan, Frederic Chopin, Steve Wozniak, Laura Bush, Roy Rogers, and Lady Gaga.[4] These people were in touch with their inner strengths and capitalized on them to impact entire generations. In most cases, it was a combination of quiet confidence and competence that gave them their strength, not their ability to spontaneously take control of a conversation.

Extroverts often have trouble leading other extroverts because they're too busy being outgoing to listen and act on everything that comes up on a team. Introverts are natural listeners and tend to respond with a calm demeanor that makes it safe for others to share.

The best introverted leaders know how to tap into both their acquired extroverted skills (which they intentionally developed) and their natural reflective tendencies. That means they can be totally themselves—and they have determined which extroverted skills they need and have worked to develop them. They don't turn into extroverts but learn how to communicate in their language (a Master Move).

Consider the outcomes of introverts using the Master Moves as we exercise our leadership skills:

- We choose our words carefully, thinking before speaking.
- We observe the dynamics of what's happening in the room.

- We capitalize on curiosity to see the big picture.
- We're willing to share credit with others and acknowledge everyone's contribution.
- We're thoughtful, reflective in what we say and what we do.
- We're more interested in a solid process than a quick win.
- We understand the value of strategy and don't rush past it.
- We're seen as diplomatic because we take time to think things through.
- We're known for our well-thought-out ideas instead of just the energy of discussing ideas.
- Our natural sincerity makes up for our quiet, non-rushed demeanor.

Also, we should recognize the barriers that can make leadership tough for introverts. Jennifer Kahnweiler, author of *The Introverted Leader*, focuses on six primary barriers that need to be addressed:

1. *People exhaustion*—We get drained faster in a high-interaction environment.
2. *A fast pace*—We feel the pressure to make decisions without time to reflect on the data.
3. *Getting interrupted*—When sharing in a group, we value taking a pause to think—but extroverts see that as a "finish" signal and jump in.
4. *Pressure to self-promote*—Bosses can't keep track of everyone's accomplishments, so it's important for introverts to make personal wins visible.
5. *An emphasis on teams*—Teams seem productive because of the energy created, but we are more productive alone.

6. *Negative impressions*—Introverts are often perceived as bored because we're not nodding in agreement.[5]

Bottom line: Who make the best leaders, extroverts or introverts? The best leaders are those who have learned how to be exactly who they are, capitalizing on their uniqueness and learning the basic skills that don't come as naturally to them. It's not about charisma or personality; it's about competence and connection. Good leaders are defined by how they handle important situations, how they motivate their team to achieve important goals, and how they inspire individuals—while being true to themselves. Writer Stacey Lastoe says,

> Be your own person and your own leader. Don't downplay your strengths just because you think they're not as important as the other personality type, and don't force yourself to work in the café area of the office where your coworkers are constantly tossing around ideas if your preference is to sit at your desk with your headphones on. You're a skilled watcher, observer, reader of situations; it'd be a deep disservice to not embrace these qualities.[6]

## Fine-Tuning Your Leadership Strengths

The most important part of leadership as an introvert is to be true to yourself. Extroverts excel at reaching out to an entire team at the same time. Introverts excel at building relationships with individuals one-on-one. Any skill that will help you do that more effectively is a skill worth mastering.

You'll probably have a variety of personalities and temperaments on your team. As an introvert, you'll be able to recognize the dynamics of what people are thinking and feeling, even when they don't express it. You'll be able to craft an environment that makes it safe for everyone to share their thoughts in their own way.

That doesn't mean the quiet ones will jump naturally into every discussion. It means that both introverts and extroverts will learn what each team member brings to the table and learn to value those unique contributions.

What's the leader's role in that process? To get to know each person as an individual to find out how that sense of safety can become a reality for them.

There's a common leadership philosophy that says you shouldn't become friends with your employees because it will make it harder to make the tough decisions when they need direction (and to keep others from thinking you're playing favorites). It's a fine line, and a challenging one. Your primary role isn't to be their best friend; it's to be their leader. That means you learn the skills needed to lead with strength and confidence, while also getting to know them as real people. You learn what's important to them outside of work, what motivates them, what challenges they're facing, and what their dreams are for their work life in the future. When you do it with sincerity instead of as a management technique, it builds trust—which becomes the foundation for their loyalty and performance.

Make an intentional effort to seek out each of your employees on a regular basis. Keep it casual and spontaneous. Instead of a formal meeting in your office, allow yourself enough margin to walk around and have a conversation with someone you pass in the hallway. Check in to see how they're doing, and follow up on anything they might have told you in previous conversations.

"How did your daughter do in that softball game a couple of weeks ago?"

"You were going to head for the hills on your vacation. Did that happen? Did you have a good time?"

"I know you were there last week for the announcement of the changes that are coming. How is that settling with you?

You're a deep processor, so I'd love to know some of your perspective, whether good or bad."

You could also send an email to your team: "I need a break. I'm going for a fifteen-minute walk at 10:00. Anybody want to join me?" You're giving them permission to pull away from work, demonstrating that it's OK to get what is needed to be effective. Don't guide the ensuing conversation; just follow their lead about whatever they want to talk about.

Take notes on these conversations, especially if anyone brings up an idea related to something the team is working on. "That's really interesting—I want to capture that so I can think on it a little more." Ponder the idea for a couple of days, then send them a text or email with a simple follow-up or clarifying question. It shows that you value their input enough to think through it and reconnect. Whether you end up using their idea or not, they'll feel valued.

During any conversation, end by summarizing what they said to make sure you've heard it correctly and understand it the way they meant it—and ask if you got it right. This shows empathy and demonstrates the deepest level of listening.

If you have a team member with a name that's unusual to you, ask them how to pronounce it correctly. Repeat it until they tell you that you've got it right. I've known leaders who mispronounced someone's name when they were hired, then continued to mispronounce it for years because they never asked (and a lot of people don't want to correct their boss). It seems like a little thing, but a person's name is part of their identity—and it means a lot to them when you want to get it right.

Sometimes, people's facial expressions don't match what they're thinking. Introverts often carry a scowl when we're thinking deeply, even if we agree with what's being presented. If you're not sure what someone is feeling, ask them privately. "I just wanted to check to see how you're feeling about what we just discussed in the meeting. You looked like you might have concerns, so I thought I'd ask."

## Team Tips

You've probably had numerous experiences being led by an extroverted boss. When you have the chance to move into leadership, it's tempting to overcompensate by leading in the way that you were missing all those years. You might structure an environment where people are encouraged to reflect and think deeply but underplay the high-energy discussions that extroverts thrive on. Doing so runs the risk of creating an environment that's introvert-friendly but alienates the needs of the extroverts.

As the leader, your job isn't to lead in the way that's most comfortable for you. It's to bring out the best in everyone you lead. Everyone brings their own genius; your challenge is to discover it, provide an environment where it can come to the surface, then nurture it so they're able to make their highest unique contribution.

That's why it's so dangerous (yet so common) to believe that leadership consists of doing a good job telling people what to do. This diminishes the creative contribution of everyone, because it makes the leader the one with the best ideas. French aviator and author Antoine de Saint-Exupéry reportedly said, "If you want to build a ship, don't drum up the men to gather wood, divide the work, and give orders. Instead, teach them to yearn for the vast and endless sea."[7]

Tell someone to build a boat and they'll build a boat. Inspire them with a vision of travel, and the possibilities of what they'll create are endless.

As much as possible, make space for both collaboration and independent work. Create a variety of work spaces that allow people to do whatever is appropriate at the moment, utilizing the resources you have. Avoid an environment that's completely open or completely isolating. Consider large and small tables in an open area where people can sit down if they want to work on something together. Create private spaces where an individual can think and work on something or collaborate with one or two others in a quiet space. Let people work from home a few days each week if possible. Encourage the use of headphones to allow isolation for thinking. One company gives noise-canceling headphones to each new employee to use when they feel it's appropriate.

Keep in mind the value that comes when introverts and extroverts collaborate in an environment that has been crafted for everyone's emotional safety. People come to recognize the value of getting a lot of ideas on the table, so extroverts become the catalyst for that initial creativity. Then there's a need to find depth and clarity around those ideas, so you can unleash and encourage the introverts to spin their magic. Everyone feels enabled to contribute through the style that's most natural for them.

### Rethinking Meetings

Someone came up with the term "death by meeting" a few years ago. It caught people's attention because of the ubiquitous experience of working in an environment where a meeting was called anytime the leader came up with an idea. Meetings can be effective, but more for extroverts than introverts. It matches the old saying, "When your only tool is a hammer, every problem becomes a nail."

As a leader, you need to get things done through people. Sometimes you'll be an informal leader, where you're leading a project team with people who don't work for you. Other times they're your direct reports. In either case, meeting together is only one way of getting their best ideas, but it can become a lazy

alternative to finding different possibilities. Consider these options for making meetings more effective or even unnecessary:

- Don't call a meeting for one issue that needs input.
  Compile issues so you can cover multiple items in one
  meeting.
- Always send out an agenda for each meeting ahead
  of time so people can prepare. It gives the introverts a
  chance to think through the ideas in preparation for the
  meeting, even if others ignore it.
- Make sure everyone in a meeting has the chance to share
  their ideas without feeling like they could be dismissed
  as irrelevant. Control the contributions of those who
  tend to monopolize the discussion so others can share.
- Encourage participants to reach out after the meeting
  in writing or in person if they have additional thoughts.
  Introverts will welcome the chance to process before
  sharing and will often be more willing to connect one-
  on-one instead of with the whole group.
- Don't assume that people will automatically share their
  thoughts in a meeting. Recognize that there is probably
  some deep thinking happening, and you'll need a variety of options for finding that information.
- Keep meetings short and on track. Maximize input
  from the quieter people by breaking participants into
  groups of two or three for about ten minutes to let
  them share, then ask one person in each team to present
  their thoughts. Introverts will feel safer sharing in that
  setting, and their ideas will come out before the whole
  group when you debrief the discussions.
- Never suggest icebreakers or calisthenics after a break
  "to get the blood flowing." It's the fastest way to clear
  the room of introverts.

Can an introvert be a wildly successful leader? Absolutely. You've got this! All it takes is a new mindset. It means using all of who you are and consistently growing your skillset to help others become all of who they are.

It means making a difference with your people and your company.

It's your strategic advantage!

# Communicating with Confidence

The single biggest problem with communication is the illusion that it has taken place.

George Bernard Shaw

I've been looking forward to this chapter because I've written so much about interpersonal communication in the past. All of my previous books have dealt with some element of it, from the foundational *How to Communicate with Confidence* to the recent *It's Better to Bite Your Tongue Than Eat Your Words.* They all came out of my own experience of being an introvert in an extrovert world. There weren't a ton of similar resources when I started, so I wrote from a combination of research plus trial and error.

I realized that a lot of people (primarily introverts) never get the tools needed for basic conversational skills. They go through life doing the best they can but don't know where to get new tools—or even that the tools exist. That's why I decided to learn everything I could, test it out, then make it available.

For this chapter, I decided to start by exploring to see what, if anything, has changed since I started writing about and researching introversion twenty years ago. I simply entered "How an introvert can learn to communicate" into a search engine, and I learned two things:

1. There are a *ton* of web pages on that topic, including popular articles, research papers, blog posts, and specialized publications.
2. There is *very little* information that is new or unique—and much of it is misleading.

It seemed that when someone wants to write about this topic, they choose one of two ways to do it:

1. They simply think about the issue and write their casual thoughts (which almost always lack the depth needed to be helpful).
2. They make the same search I did, then copy the ideas others have written, change the wording, and publish the same content.

That second one threw me off the most. I was amazed at how similar the content was in dozens of articles I looked through. I'm not sure who came up with the original ideas, but everyone's bullet points seemed to match. I don't want to say that people stole someone else's idea, but I think it's safe to say there wasn't much original thinking. The major points were on target; they were just repeated and repackaged. I wanted to do better by finding fresh insights and perspectives.

## Communication Tool Kit

For this chapter, I decided to share my own introvert's perspective based on what I've learned over the years. Some of these ideas have been mentioned in earlier chapters, and all of them tie into one or more Master Moves. Together, they form a primer on how to best communicate as an introvert.

### 1. Believe you have something of value to offer.

When we understand how unique our strengths are and how deeply we can process and present information, we won't need to compare ourselves to others. People may not turn to us for *quick* answers, but they will seek us out when they want *well-thought-through* perspectives.

### 2. Pick the right environment to talk.

When I've been invited to meet someone at a noisy restaurant, staying engaged in that environment feels like swimming uphill. If I have to strain to hear what the other person is saying, my energy disappears quickly.

I've learned to suggest an alternative location and tell the other person why. Likewise, if someone in the office wants to talk through something that requires focus, I'll say, "Great— let's duck into this empty conference room where it's a little quieter."

### 3. Learn to ask good questions.

Of all the tools introverts have, asking good questions is the granddaddy of them all. It's tough to think of what to say when the conversation lags, which is why we often dread silence. Having the ability to formulate questions based on what the other person just said is a secret weapon when it's used honestly— not as a gimmick to keep things moving but as an expression of genuine curiosity.

### 4. Be confident in being yourself—while always growing and building your skills.

We can use our self-confidence to progress, improve, and learn new skills. This ties in with the Japanese business concept of *kaizen*, or "continuous improvement." Books and resources over the past few years have been written to help introverts accept who we are. Such resources are a perfect place to start, but then we need to focus on learning new and different communication skills to interact with and influence others.

### 5. Listen and observe actively, not passively.

It's common for introverts to ignore the need to use more facial expression and reactions when we're listening. Without facial cues, people can think we're either disengaged or arrogant.

It's a simple fix and just takes practice. Learn to make good eye contact; nod often when you're understanding what's being said; smile when you hear something you identify with, and drop in verbal cues like "Crazy, right?" or "I hear you," or "Makes sense." Show that you are actively listening.

### 6. Take breaks as needed.

If my car's gas tank is only half the size of yours, I'll need to stop more often to refill. No amount of wishing will change that, and if I try to keep driving on an empty tank, I'll stall out.

The same thing is true in conversations. If you've been in high-energy conversations for a while, even when they're going well, you can tell when you're running low on fuel. Take a break to recharge—and don't apologize. In some cases, it might be as simple as saying, "Interesting! Give me a second. I need to think about that before I respond." Other times, it could mean visiting the restroom (whether you need to or not) just to clear your head, or skipping that next meeting if you can.

Doing your best critical work requires fuel. For introverts, alone time is essential, not optional.

### 7. Make what you say count.

In any situation, whether it's a team meeting, a virtual call, a conversation with a colleague, or a transaction with a client or customer, it's important to make what you say count. Your words can add value and help make you visible—but only if you have something worthwhile to contribute. If you say only one thing during each encounter, make it count. That's what introverts do well.

If you feel like you should talk more, ask yourself if it's because you have more value to add (then add it) or if it's to stay visible like the extroverts (then don't add it). Always be selective in what you share. Think quality over quantity. The more concise you can be, the more impact your words will have. Fluff always dilutes impact.

### 8. Prepare for every encounter.

Preparation is a critical introvert skill for navigating any conversation (which is why it's a Master Move). Always ask yourself, *What's the purpose of this encounter?*

- If it's lunch with a friend, review the things you know are happening in their life or things you've talked about recently to keep them top of mind.
- If it's a conversation with a customer who walks into your location, remind yourself that you don't know everything that's going on in their life. Approach them with kindness, and you'll give them the gift of genuine caring that builds a human connection.
- If it's a team meeting, grab the agenda ahead of time and decide what your perspective is on each item so you can contribute as appropriate.

- If you're in a service industry, listen to requests carefully, ask questions to clarify, then meet their needs with precision. Always be grateful that you have the opportunity to serve someone and make a difference in their life.
- If it's a connection with your boss, think through your side of the agenda (if there is one), as well as an appropriate question or two about how they're doing as a person. "I know that latest change in the compensation structure has everybody on edge. How's it affecting you?" You're not trying to be nosy; just finding genuine ways to care.

### 9. Build on individual relationships.

In most types of work, you can't avoid occasional large group gatherings—but they drain your energy faster than small groups. Attend and take part, but always try to follow up and engage at the smallest level possible. It might take longer, but you're building relationships where you can go much deeper.

When someone shares something that concerns you in a meeting, don't review it with others after the meeting is over—that turns into gossip. Think carefully through your concerns, find the simplest possible way to express them, and go directly to that person and ask questions. "I heard what you said in the meeting," you could say, "and it was interesting and different from what I was thinking. I'd like to hear more about what you're thinking and see how it fits with the ideas I had."

You'll do your best work one-on-one or in the smallest possible groups. Gravitate toward those as much as possible and use larger meetings for active listening and observation.

## Conversation Hacks for Introverts

There are a number of things we can do to learn to excel in conversation. Let's review a few hacks—first for connecting with individuals, then for connecting in front of a group.

### Connect with individuals.

*Preparation is the best Master Move an introvert can use to feel confident in conversations.* When you feel confident, you don't have to have an answer for everything you're asked. It gives you the ability to say "I don't know" without feeling intimidated and gains the respect of others when you're able to do so.

*Be constantly on the lookout for ways to affirm your coworkers.* If they bring up a valuable perspective in a meeting, take a few seconds to let them know. "When you responded to Kevin's comment in that meeting this morning, I was really impressed by the way you positioned your thoughts. It calmed everything down and took the discussion in a new direction. That was impressive!" Never make things up to flatter someone. Always keep it genuine—but if you feel it, say it. It doesn't take much to give somebody a boost for their day, and it builds trust in your relationship.

*Even if it's one of your executives or managers who makes a great decision, or has the courage to make a tough one, let them know with a quick thank-you email.* Just a couple of sentences that say, "That was refreshing," or "That was tough—thanks for being willing to make the hard calls" are worth sending. Leaders are human, and humans respond well to genuine kindness.

*Develop keen curiosity.* Assume that every person you talk to knows something you don't—and it's your job to find out what it is. Ask clarifying questions and make fewer statements in every conversation. Have a mindset of exploration.

*If you have to have a tough conversation, consider going for a walk with the other person.* If you're walking side by side, you won't have as much eye contact. Usually, you want a lot of it, but it can be easier to talk about some things if you're not looking directly at them—and walking makes it a more casual conversation.

### Connect in front of groups.

Comedian Jerry Seinfeld said, "According to most studies, people's number one fear is public speaking. Number two is death. . . . This means to the average person, if you go to a funeral, you're better off in the casket than doing the eulogy."[1]

No matter what our job, there may be times when we're asked to present before a group. It might be our work team or the entire organization—or even the media. This is often the place where introverts do some of our best work.

We don't like to be surprised by being called up in front of a group, because we don't know what will happen or what we should say. We might freeze up because we think everyone else is critiquing us, which probably isn't true. However, if introverts are given an assignment to present before a group and plenty of time to prepare, it's often where we shine. We pull information together and synthesize it in a way that's easy for people to understand. We come across as confident and simple.

I'm exactly that way. Put me in front of a room with plenty of prep time, and I'm excited and confident. I'm in charge, and I know what's going to happen. But put me in a meeting where someone might call me up front and I don't know what's going to happen, and I'm way out of my comfort zone.

When you're leading a session, here are a few ways to capitalize on the opportunity:

*If someone asks a question and you can't think of a quick response, be honest and deflect.* "That's a great question. I'll answer it, but I need to think about it for a minute. Let's get some input from a few of you while I'm processing, and I'll share my thoughts after that, OK?" You're not avoiding the question; you're promising to answer while honoring your need to process briefly.

*If you're in a meeting and the leader asks for input on something, go first.* There's usually a pause before the first person speaks, so it's the perfect time to add value, and it's easier than trying to jump in later.

*When sharing your thoughts, "pre-number" your ideas.* When sharing several ideas, introverts often pause slightly between ideas to regroup for the next thought. The danger is that someone sees that pause as a "finished" sign and jumps in. However, if you begin with "I've got three quick thoughts on that. Number one . . ." and someone tries to jump in, it's easier to say, "Hang on—let me finish my thoughts so I don't forget them."

## You Can Excel at Communication

You can excel at communication. Why? Because you're an introvert. If you tap into your unique strengths as an introvert, you can be the most powerful communicator in the room.

In any conversation. With anyone. At any time.

You'll be at your best, because you'll help others be their best through your ideas and words.

You'll truly enjoy the journey!

18

# Focusing on a Greater Purpose

The meaning of life is to find your gift. The purpose of life is to give it away.

Pablo Picasso

Several years ago, my wife and I attended a Renaissance faire, an outdoor event that replicates life during medieval times with jousting competitions, fair maidens, period costumes, and tourists walking around gnawing on roasted turkey legs. We saw craftspeople in booths hawking their handmade jewelry, artwork, clothing, and trinkets while calling out loud greetings to passersby: "Good morrow, thou strapping young lad—well met!"

One section of the faire included rustic games. For a few coins, you could test your skill in competitive games like Ax Throwing, Oaf Bag Toss, Bump a Monk, or Toss Your Cookies. We were mostly amused as we strolled past the noisy booths.

But one game caught my attention: The Rat Race.

It was a crude wooden maze, sitting vertically on a table about four feet high. There were four compartments at the bottom with hinged doors, and a cage sat off to one side with about a dozen rats inside. Each rat was a different color or had unique markings, and four competitors could select which rat they wanted to use in the competition.

I couldn't resist. I paid my coins, picked my rat, and waited anxiously. The host of the booth brought our rats to us and introduced us by name. My rat was Winston.

The host then put the selected rats in the hinged boxes at the bottom. On a signal, a worker would remove a board, freeing the rats to climb the maze to get the food treat waiting at the top.

The energetic host whipped the crowd with cheers for each rat: "Huzzah for Winston!" That lasted several minutes, which turned out to be just a little too long for Winston.

The game started. The board was removed, and three rats raced to the top.

Winston had fallen asleep in his box.

*I lost the rat race.*

My consolation prize was a small, ancient-looking piece of paper with the words, "I LOST THE RAT RACE." I kept that paper in my wallet for a long time as a reminder. It was surprisingly true.

People—introverts and extroverts alike—get caught up in the rat race, trying to get ahead at work and make their mark in life. We compete with each other and forsake our values, health, and sanity for the sake of profit and status.

But it's the wrong race. It's the rat race.

And nobody gets out of it alive.

Don't get me wrong; I'm all for achieving great purposes and reaching goals that make an impact. I'm passionate about helping people get "unstuck" in life and make a difference. That's what I do for a living. But that's a different race.

When we find ourselves running the rat race, we become addicted to adrenaline. It's movement without purpose. It's making progress without making a difference.

Nobody wins the rat race. But we can easily get caught up in it and not even realize what's happening. It's not that different from rats that jump into a wheel and start running. They exert lots of energy but never go anywhere.

## What Matters Most?

Back in the 1960s, a Senate committee heard expert testimony on time management. The researcher suggested that because of all the time-saving advances in technology, things would look radically different in twenty years. Workers would have to cut back dramatically on how many hours they worked each week, or how many weeks they worked each year. Most would have to retire earlier than planned. One of the biggest challenges for people would be figuring out what to do with all their spare time.[1]

Sixty years later, we see three significant outcomes:

1. Technology that saves time has expanded exponentially since the 1960s.
2. We're busier and more rushed and more stressed than ever because that technology has crept into every corner of our lives.
3. Introverts can be more susceptible because they feel the effects more deeply than others.

Right? When's the last time you felt like you had enough time to get everything done that you felt you needed to accomplish? Is your life characterized by hurry—even in little things that don't need to be rushed? As we pull up to a red light, we see there is one car in each lane ahead of us. Based on the make and model of each car, we try to guess which one will pull away the fastest when the light changes so we can get behind them (and we're frustrated if we pick the slower one). Or we try to pick the fastest checkout lane at the grocery store based on the number of carts in each lane, as well as how full the carts are.

Author and pastor John Ortberg wrote, "Hurry is not just a disordered schedule; hurry is a disordered heart."[2] He suggests that we have "traded wisdom for information. We have exchanged depth for breadth. We want to microwave maturity."[3]

Dr. Steven R. Covey wrote about the importance of knowing where you want to end up so your choices move you in the right direction. "It's incredibly easy to get caught up in an activity trap, in the busyness of life, to work harder and harder at climbing the ladder of success only to discover it's leaning against the wrong wall."[4]

We're trying to win the rat race.

Toddlers innocently give us the right question here: "Why?" Why do we get caught up so easily in the high expectations of performance? Is it because we want to be successful at work, or because that's our resource for building a fulfilling life? It's easy to justify overachievement because it "pays the bills," so it's critical to step back and get a clear picture of where work fits into our entire life.

Dr. Covey used to teach people to write the eulogy they wanted read at their funeral. At first, it would seem like a gruesome assignment, but it was designed to help people focus on what mattered most in their lives so they wouldn't miss it. It's a great exercise for clarifying perspective so that one's career becomes a meaningful tool in building a life that matters—but not the only tool. For introverts, it's especially valuable since we have a natural inclination for deep, reflective thinking.

Over the years, I've known people who I felt were indispensable to a company. I couldn't imagine them not being there because they were such an integral part of the organization.

Then they announced they had taken another position with a different employer.

Within a week, their job was posted on appropriate sites, and we were taking applications. Then their position was filled, and we had to adjust to someone doing the job differently. We compared and complained but eventually adjusted and moved forward. Soon, we weren't even thinking about the former employee much because we were too busy getting things done.

We work hard to accomplish great things at work. But at our funeral, nobody will remember those things. They'll remember how we made them feel. If that's true, it should inform how we make choices about where to focus and how to balance our lives.

## What's That Have to Do with Introverts?

Why are we talking about this in a book about how introverts thrive in the workplace? Because the workplace often becomes a catalyst for hurrying and rushing and stressing in order to perform in a way that gets stellar results. Instead, we can become experts at capitalizing on our unique introvert skills and navigating the extroverted work environment where we find ourselves. We can thrive, and we can succeed. We can take everything we've learned in this book and move to the highest levels of impact and influence. We become powerful, effective introverts.

All the while, if we forget to pay attention to the rest of our lives, we may end up racing down a path of eventual regret. Someone said that when we're on our deathbed, none of us will say, "I wish I had spent more time at the office." That's why we're pausing in this chapter to make sure we're doing everything for the right reasons.

This applies to everyone, not just introverts—but we tend to be more susceptible to the danger. We're keenly aware (more than we should be) of how others perceive us. Introverts usually have some people-pleasing tendencies, so we try even harder to succeed and get a good response from others. It's tougher for us; we simultaneously have to learn how to get comfortable with who we are while honing the skills of interacting with others.

Extroverts are usually energized in high-stimulation situations. They like being around other people and gain energy from those encounters. If they learn to focus on what matters most to them in the long term, they have the natural energy to take them there. If they don't, it's tough for them to decide on what goals are most important to them and move toward them.

In contrast, introverts get natural energy when we're alone. We can apply our skills of interacting in a workplace, but it doesn't give us more energy; it uses energy and depletes it—and we need alone time to recharge. When that energy is present, choosing important life goals becomes motivating. Introverts are motivated by deep purpose, and it gives us a reason to find that restoration whenever it's needed.

For both extroverts and introverts, there has to be something ahead that has so much personal value that it's worth the effort to keep after it. When we find that "something," we've found the right race to run.

## Don't Get Stuck

You picked this book up to become more effective in the workplace. But if you master all seven moves yet have no sense of purpose that energizes you, there's no real benefit. Everything you do should move you closer to who you want to be in your life.

That's the reason behind everything we've explored here. You can be 100 percent "you," 100 percent of who you want to be, and never have to try to become something you're not.

There's one final question to explore: How do we keep from slipping back into old perspectives and behaviors? When we're healthy and energized, it's not a problem. But if we're tired or caught in boredom or feel like we're in a rut, it's natural for introverts to revert to old ways of thinking. *I'll always be an introvert*, we think. *So I'll always be limited in what I can do.*

That's a victim mentality. If we see ourselves as victims, it means somebody else is calling the shots. We believe there are limits on what we can do because we're victims of our circumstances—or in this case, our temperament. We stop reaching out for the things we're passionate about. A victim mentality says, "Someone or something is in the way of my success and happiness, and there's nothing I can do about it."

Fortunately, we have an alternative: being *proactive*.

Being proactive is the opposite of being reactive. Instead of reacting to the things that happen in our lives, we take the initiative to find a positive outcome. In most cases, being proactive means we take action to change the things we have control over and learn to accept and adapt to the things we can't control.

Remember the Serenity Prayer? Richard Niebuhr wrote, "God grant me the serenity to accept the things I cannot change; courage to change the things I can; and the wisdom to know the difference."[5] Let's unpack that, because it's the key to success in work and life.

### Accept what we cannot change.

As I'm writing this, the temperature in Southern California is about as hot as it ever gets—in the hundreds. My wife and I don't like heat, which is why we moved here several decades ago after eleven years in Phoenix (where it can hit 118 degrees during the summer). We usually go north for cool vacations, not south for sunny ones. It's tough for me to keep a good attitude when it's blazing hot outside. I could let the weather ruin my whole week and be discouraged and angry about the heat, but there's nothing I can do about it. I don't want to be a victim of the weather—something I can't change. Instead, I've been intentional about accepting the heat as a temporary fact of life, and I find creative ways to adapt. Rather than writing outside on the patio, I'll go to an air-conditioned coffee shop so I can focus. I also plan my outdoor exercise for right after sunrise instead of waiting until later in the day.

Our everyday inner peace is directly related to our ability to accept what we cannot change. When we hold on to anger or frustration about what we don't have control of, we become victims of those people or circumstances. In a real sense, we've surrendered control of our emotions—and we're stuck and can't move forward. Accepting the things that we can't control gives us freedom, redirecting the energy we're spending on frustration into investing in positive outcomes.

### Have the courage to change what we can.

What can be changed? Well, I'm an introvert. I'll never be an extrovert, and it would be pointless to try to become one. Instead, I've learned to treasure my introversion and capitalize on it. At the same time, I know that I can gain new skills to help me function well in situations where extroversion is valued.

It would be easy for us to just say, "I'm an introvert, so I'll just settle into that. There's no need to grow." That's why it takes courage to realize that while our temperament stays the same, our skills can change. That's the secret to effectiveness as introverts at work—choosing a mindset of constant growth and skill development. We don't have to become the smoothest communicator in the room, but we can gain skills that significantly increase our contribution and confidence at work.

### Gain the wisdom to know the difference.

Perhaps having the wisdom to know what we can and cannot change doesn't seem too hard, but it can be deceptive. It's easy to assume that certain things don't need to change because they're in our comfort zone (and have always been there). It takes intentionality, first to notice and become aware of those things, and then to challenge them. Are they permanent, or is there something we could do to grow in that area?

Becoming proactive can change everything in our workplace, and also in our life outside of work. We can choose not to be victims of the people we encounter, whether we work with them, do business with them, or live with them. When we make that choice, we're controlling the only thing we can control—ourselves.

And when we do, we have a credible claim to the rich, fulfilling, and rewarding life of an introvert.

# A FINAL PERSPECTIVE
# FOR INTROVERTS

Here's what we've learned in this book:

- It's not an extrovert's world, even if it feels like it. There are just about as many of us as there are of them.
- Some people work in jobs where extrovert skills stand out (like sales). But when introverts are passionate about these jobs, we can learn to do them with excellence when we tap into our uniqueness.
- Some people work in teams that have more extroverts than introverts. But we can make a deep contribution nobody else can make.
- Everyone has skills they're both stronger and weaker in. We all need to grow and gain new skills.
- Extroverts aren't better than introverts, and introverts aren't better than extroverts. We're just different—and each of us brings unique contributions that are critical for the success of any organization.
- We're all on a journey of becoming our best selves.

- Companies don't need more extroverts; they need every unique individual bringing their best selves to work every day.

Introverts may have had the perception that to succeed in business, we need to become someone else to function in a workplace that places value on extrovert skills. As we've discovered in the book, that's not the case. Whether it's a corporate situation or an entrepreneurial endeavor, we have everything we need to be wildly successful when we tap into the unique strengths that make up our temperament. We don't have to become extroverts. We just need to be fully present and claim our spot in the workplace.

We'll thrive when we can master two things:

1. Fully understanding the world of the extrovert so we can learn what it takes to work with precision in that environment.
2. Fully mastering the world of the introvert so we can capitalize on our own unique strengths in order to make the greatest possible contribution.

This is a book about hope. It's not about *survival*; it's about *celebrating* and *cultivating* our uniqueness as introverts. It's about being a victor, not a victim. It's about building on our introvert strengths and gaining the additional skills needed to thrive in every work environment. That happens to the degree that we quit trying to become extroverts and fully embrace who we are.

It's where the magic happens.

My goal has been to nudge you toward a clearer picture of your purpose and how you can succeed in every part of your life. Decide where you're going and take your own life journey, not someone else's journey. Then use your natural temperament and grow your skills to get there.

At the end of your life, you won't win the rat race. Nobody wins that race. Don't waste your life trying to be something you're not. Focus on becoming and offering the best version of yourself.

That's how you make a difference in the world!

# ACKNOWLEDGMENTS

Writing a book is like hiking the Grand Canyon for the first time. It's a very romantic idea, and you're excited to start the journey. But then you realize you have to hike back to the top, and it's uphill all the way. You get sweaty and tired and grumpy and wish you could quit—but you have to make it to the end. If you do it alone, it's miserable. If you do it with a group of friends, it's still work—but they give you the encouragement to keep going, and you're all doing it together.

Every author gets a page to "acknowledge" the people who went on the journey with them—the ones without whom the author might have given up. It's always my favorite page to write, because it's a chance to say "Thanks—you're amazing" to those amazing people. But it's also a chance to slow down and check out the sunrise and feel grateful that I've even had the chance to do this journey at all. What a privilege!

This is my ninth time hiking this literary canyon. As I look back, I realize that many of the same people have been with me on all of these trips, with an occasional newbie hiking along. That makes it familiar and comfortable, and I'm grateful we've learned to operate as a team that gets better with each trip.

You could probably read the Acknowledgments page in all of my previous books and see the same names appearing. That's a good thing, and we're all a lot more seasoned than we were at the beginning.

My wife, Diane, is always at the top of my list. You'd think that after forty-six years, it would get routine, and we'd take each other for granted. But it's still fresh. I never know what to expect, and she's still the best decision I ever made. Those kinds of relationships change because they grow—and we're still growing. It's deeper. It's better. And it's a whole lot of fun. We're going for forty-six more.

Vicki Crumpton has edited every book I've written, which is the only reason they're worth reading. I'm always in awe of her ability to take my stumbling ideas and words and make them simple and coherent. Simply stated, she has mentored me to become a real writer.

In my last book, I said, "If Vicki ever retires, you'll probably stop buying my books. She's that good." I guess that was prophetic because she retired shortly after that. The good news is that I met her replacement, Rachel McRae, several years ago, and I didn't know that much energy and competence could exist in a single package. She's my new editor, and I've been thrilled to get to work with her these past few months. She's the newbie on the trail this time out, but I think she brings the best trail mix. (The best news is that Vicki got to take one more hike down the canyon and did the editing on this book.)

Revell (a division of Baker Publishing Group) has become more than my publisher. They've become my "home." I've settled in with them for the long haul, and it's grown into a high trust relationship. If I ever get stuck on the trail, I'm convinced they'll send donkeys.

As for the other traveling companions, the group includes my family members, friends, and colleagues who do life with me. That means they hike with me because they care, and they have more influence over my thinking than anyone else. Tim and his wife, Lucy, Sara and her hubby, Brian, and the amazing grandkids they've given me bring sheer joy and purpose into my life. Friends like Jeremy, Glenn, Lana, Paul, Vickie, and a bunch of others keep me challenged, and fellow writers like Jessica and Lex keep me encouraged.

I could probably include everybody I've encountered, because every conversation shapes my thinking. But there's not room, and I know I'd forget someone.

My life and career and the chance to make a little impact through writing are gifts from God. He's my reason I get to do any of this, and I get to enjoy a personal relationship with him. He knows the trail well because he made the canyon, so he's the best hiking companion ever.

For that, I'm eternally grateful.

# NOTES

## Introduction

1. Mohit Parikh, "Invention Story: Noise Cancelling Headphones," Engineers Garage, accessed February 28, 2023, https://www.engineersgarage.com/invention-story-noise-cancelling-headphones/.

2. Jenn Granneman, "There Might Not Be as Many Extroverts in the World as We Think, Science Says," *Introvert, Dear* (blog), April 9, 2015, https://introvertdear.com/news/there-might-not-be-as-many-extroverts-in-the-world-as-we-think-science-says/.

## Chapter 1 Where the Journey Began

1. Dictionary.com, s.v. "introvert," accessed February 28, 2023, https://www.dictionary.com/browse/introvert.

2. Stephen R. Covey, *The 7 Habits of Highly Effective People*, thirtieth anniversary edition (New York: Simon & Schuster, 2020), 18–20.

3. Jonathan Rauch, "Caring for Your Introvert," *Atlantic*, March 2003, https://www.theatlantic.com/magazine/archive/2003/03/caring-for-your-introvert/302696/.

## Part 1 Introverts at Work

1. Sarah Lambersky, "How to Manage Your 40,000 Negative Thoughts a Day and Keep Moving Forward," *Financial Post*, October 16, 2013, https://financialpost.com/entrepreneur/three-techniques-to-manage-40000-negative-thoughts.

## Chapter 2 The Introvert Revival

1. William Pannapacker, "Screening Out the Introverts," *Chronicle of Higher Education*, April 15, 2012, https://www.chronicle.com/article/screening-out-the-introverts/.

2. Scott Barry Kaufman, "What Kind of Introvert Are You?" *Beautiful Minds* (blog), September 29, 2014, https://blogs.scientificamerican.com/beauti ful-minds/what-kind-of-introvert-are-you/.

3. Susan Cain, as quoted in NJ Lechnir, "The Most Interesting Research You'll Ever Find about Introverts," *The Frog Blog* (blog), February 6, 2019, https://leapfroggingsuccess.com/most-interesting-research-ever-intro verts/.

4. Marti Olsen Laney, *The Introvert Advantage: How to Thrive in an Extrovert World* (New York: Workman Publishing, 2002), 6.

5. Maggie Zahn, "How to Become So Good They Can't Ignore You," *Business Insider*, July 17, 2014, https://www.businessinsider.com/become-so -good-they-cant-ignore-you-2014-7.

## Chapter 3 Mind Games

1. Matt Grawitch, "Biases Are Neither All Good Nor All Bad," *Psychology Today*, September 10, 2020, https://www.psychologytoday.com/us/blog/hov ercraft-full-eels/202009/biases-are-neither-all-good-nor-all-bad.

2. Julia Carter, "Tackling Introversion Bias in the Workplace," Zestfor, accessed January 26, 2023, https://www.zestfor.com/tackling-introversion -bias-in-the-workplace/.

3. Carter, "Tackling Introversion Bias."

4. Carter, "Tackling Introversion Bias."

5. Kathy Caprino, "Do You Have a Bias against Introverts? I Did, and I'm Ashamed of It," *The Finding Brave Newsletter*, July 23 2021, https://www .linkedin.com/pulse/do-you-have-bias-against-introverts-i-did-im-ashamed -kathy-caprino/.

## Chapter 4 Myth Busters

1. Heidi Kasevich, "It's Not Just Gender Holding You Back," *Huffpost*, February 22, 2017, https://www.huffpost.com/entry/its-not-just-gender-hol ding-you-back_b_589deaece4b0e172783a9b4b.

2. Adam M. Grant, Francesca Gino, and David A. Hoffman, "Reversing the Extraverted Leadership Advantage: The Role of Employee Proactivity," *Academy of Management Journal* 54, no. 3 (June 2011): 528–50, https://journals .aom.org/doi/abs/10.5465/amj.2011.61968043.

3. As quoted in "60 Inspirational Harvey Mackay Quotes (TIME)," Gracious, September 13, 2022, https://graciousquotes.com/harvey-mackay/.

4. Keith Ferrazzi, *Never Eat Alone* (New York: Doubleday, 2005), 8.

5. As quoted in Dan Western, "30 Keith Farrazzi Quotes from *Never Eat Alone*," Wealthy Gorilla, July 18, 2022, https://wealthygorilla.com/keith -ferrazzi-quotes/.

6. Western, "30 Keith Ferrazzi Quotes."

7. Fiona MacDonald, "The Science of Introverts vs Extroverts," Science Alert, October 24, 2016, https://www.sciencealert.com/the-science-of-intro verts-vs-extroverts.

8. Jenn Granneman, "10 Signs Your Baby (or Toddler) Is an Introvert," *Psychology Today*, January 29, 2019, https://www.psychologytoday.com/us/blog /the-secret-lives-introverts/201901/10-signs-your-baby-or-toddler-is-introvert.

9. Amy Simpson, "Confessions of a Ministry Introvert," *Christian Living Books* (blog), April 3, 2018, https://christianlivingbooks.com/confessions-of -a-ministry-introvert/.

10. Heather McColloch, "Embracing the Introverted Brain," *Mind Brain Ed Think Tank+* (blog), February 2020, https://www.mindbrained.org/2020 /02/embracing-the-introverted-brain/#.

## Chapter 5 How to Talk to Yourself

1. Marina Krakovsky, "The Self-Compassion Solution" (white paper), *The Introvert Entrepreneur*, May–June 2017, https://theintrovertentrepreneur.com /wp-content/uploads/2014/01/Self-Compassion.pdf.

2. Shad Helmstetter, *What to Say When You Talk to Yourself* (New York: Gallery Books, 1986), 10–11.

3. Helmstetter, *What to Say When You Talk to Yourself*, 10–11.

4. As quoted in Robert Wolgemuth, *Gun Lap: Staying in the Race with Purpose* (Nashville: B&H Books, 2021), 60.

5. As quoted in "80 Moving On Quotes That Will Help You Let Go," *Reader's Digest*, November 23, 2021, https://www.rd.com/article/moving-on -quotes/.

6. Adam Grant (@AdamMGrant), Instagram post, February 21, 2022, https://www.instagram.com/p/CaQDRpTvF-m/.

7. Grant, Instagram post, February 21, 2022.

8. As quoted in Polly Campbell, "Positive Self-Talk Can Help You Win the Race—Or the Day," *Psychology Today*, June 14, 2011, https://www.psy chologytoday.com/us/blog/imperfect-spirituality/201106/positive-self-talk -can-help-you-win-the-race-or-the-day.

9. Inner Drive, "6 Ways to Improve How You Talk to Yourself," *Inner Drive* (blog), accessed January 27, 2023, https://blog.innerdrive.co.uk/6-ways -to-improve-how-you-talk-to-yourself.

## Part 2 The Seven Master Moves

1. As quoted in Vivek Ranadive and Kevin Maney, *The Two-Second Advantage: How We Succeed by Anticipating the Future—Just Enough* (London: Hodder, 2011), 3.

2. Charles McGrath, "Elders on Ice," *New York Times*, March 13, 1997, https://www.nytimes.com/1997/03/23/magazine/elders-on-ice.html.

## Chapter 6  Learning to Speak Extrovert

1. As quoted in John Worne, "Languages—Getting to the Heart," *USC Center on Public Diplomacy* (blog), December 6, 2013, https://uscpublicdiplomacy.org/blog/languages-getting-hearts.

2. Hidaya Aliouche, "The Impact of Learning a Language on Brain Health" (white paper), News Medical Life Sciences, February 15, 2022, https://www.news-medical.net/health/The-Impact-of-Learning-a-Language-on-Brain-Health.aspx.

## Chapter 7  Managing Energy for Peak Performance

1. "Earl Nightingale Quotes," Quote Fancy, accessed January 30, 2023, https://quotefancy.com/quote/797743/Earl-Nightingale-Whatever-the-majority-of-people-is-doing-under-any-given-circumstances.

2. Stephen R. Covey, *First Things First* (1994; repr. New York: Free Press, 2003), 103.

3. Ivelisse Estrada, "Sheena Iyengar: Choosy about Choosing," *Harvard Gazette*, October 22, 2010, https://news.harvard.edu/gazette/story/newsplus/sheena-iyengar-choosy-about-choosing/.

4. As quoted in Jeff Goins, *Real Artists Don't Starve: Timeless Strategies for Thriving in the New Creative Age* (New York: HarperCollins, 2017), 192.

## Chapter 8  Creating Influence through Gentle Persuasion

1. Kate Jones, "A Practical Guide to Influence for Introverts," *Better Humans* (blog), June 5, 2017, https://betterhumans.pub/a-practical-guide-to-influence-for-introverts-25da18924141.

2. As quoted in Jones, "Practical Guide to Influence."

3. Jones, "Practical Guide to Influence."

4. Holley Gerth, "What You Need to Know about Introverts and Influence," Introvert Spring, accessed January 30, 2023, https://introvertspring.com/what-you-need-to-know-about-introverts-and-influence/.

5. Jeff Hyman, "The Best Talkers Might Not Be Your Best Performers," *Forbes*, August 14, 2018, https://www.forbes.com/sites/jeffhyman/2018/08/14/introverts/?sh=7a4da3f227dd.

## Chapter 9  Building Trust

1. Macmillan Dictionary, s.v. "trust," accessed January 30, 2023, https://www.macmillandictionary.com/us/dictionary/american/trust_1.

## Chapter 10  Nurturing Emotional Intelligence

1. Daniel Goleman, "What Makes a Leader?" *Harvard Business Review*, January 2004, https://hbr.org/2004/01/what-makes-a-leader.

2. Goleman, "What Makes a Leader?"

3. Goleman, "What Makes a Leader?"

4. NPR, "Americans Flunk Self-Assessment," *All Things Considered*, October 6, 2007, https://www.npr.org/templates/story/story.php?storyId=1 5073430.

5. Ken Blanchard, "Feedback Is the Breakfast of Champions," *Ken Blanchard Books* (blog), August 17, 2009, https://www.kenblanchardbooks.com/feedback-is-the-breakfast-of-champions/.

## Chapter 11 Customizing Your Work Environment

1. As quoted in Lillian Cunningham, "Office Design for Introverts, by an Introvert," *Washington Post*, June 4, 2014, https://www.washingtonpost.com/news/on-leadership/wp/2014/06/04/office-design-for-introverts-by-an-introvert/.

2. As quoted in Paul Gallagher, "The Complete Introvert's Guide to Surviving an Open-Plan Office," *The Startup* (blog), August 26, 2019, https://medium.com/swlh/the-complete-introverts-guide-to-surviving-an-open-plan-office-f21a5e1072c2.

## Chapter 12 Ensuring Success through Intentional Preparation

1. "Abraham Lincoln Quotes," Goodreads, accessed January 31, 2023, https://www.goodreads.com/quotes/83633-give-me-six-hours-to-chop-down-a-tree-and.

2. "Albert Einstein Quotes," Goodreads, accessed January 31, 2023, https://www.goodreads.com/quotes/60780-if-i-had-an-hour-to-solve-a-problem-i-d.

3. "Stephen R. Covey Quotes," Goodreads, accessed January 31, 2023, https://www.goodreads.com/quotes/1017494-have-you-ever-been-too-busy-driving-to-take-time.

4. Patrick Carroll et al., "Feeling Prepared Increases Confidence in Any Accessible Thoughts Affecting Evaluation Unrelated to the Original Domain of Preparation," *Journal of Experimental Social Psychology* 89 (July 2020), https://www.sciencedirect.com/science/article/abs/pii/S002210311930 4780.

5. Roger Crawford, "The Power of Preparation," *Roger Crawford Blog* (blog), accessed February 1, 2023, https://rogercrawford.com/blog/the-power-of-preparation/.

## Chapter 13 Crafting Your Career

1. Emma Featherstone, "How Extroverts Are Taking the Top Jobs—and What Introverts Can Do about It," *Guardian*, February 23, 2018, https://www.theguardian.com/business-to-business/2018/feb/23/how-extroverts-are-taking-the-top-jobs-and-what-introverts-can-do-about-it.

## Chapter 15 Becoming Visible

1. Annie Nova, "Dread Going Back to the Office? Therapists Share Tips on How to Readjust," CNBC, October 25, 2021, https://www.cnbc.com/2021/10/25/what-to-do-if-youre-anxious-about-returning-to-the-office-.html.

2. Ronald S. Burt, "Structural Holes and Good Ideas," *American Journal of Sociology* 110, no. 2 (September 2004): 349–99, https://www.jstor.org/stable/10.1086/421787#metadata_info_tab_contents.

## Chapter 16 Leading Your People

1. As quoted in Larry Osborne, *Lead Like a Shepherd* (Nashville: Thomas Nelson, 2018), 133.

2. Jason Gots, "Of Lemmings and Leadership (with Jim Collins)," Big Think, November 17, 2011, https://bigthink.com/personal-growth/of-lemmings-and-leadership-with-jim-collins/.

3. Jim Collins, "Charisma, Schmarisma: Real Leaders Are Zealots," Big Think, accessed February 1, 2023, https://bigthink.com/videos/charisma-schmarisma-real-leaders-are-zealots/.

4. John Rampton, "23 of the Most Amazingly Successful Introverts in History," *Inc.*, July 20, 2015, https://www.inc.com/john-rampton/23-amazingly-successful-introverts-throughout-history.html.

5. Jennifer B. Kahnweiler, *The Introverted Leader: Building on Your Quiet Strength* (Oakland, CA: Berrett-Koehler Publishers, 2018), 28–30.

6. Stacey Lastoe, "3 Things Introverts Can Do to Thrive in an Extroverted Workplace," The Muse, accessed February 2, 2023, https://www.themuse.com/advice/3-things-introverts-can-do-to-thrive-in-an-extroverted-workplace.

7. As quoted in Richard Bolden, "A Yearning for the Vast and Endless Sea: From Competence to Purpose in Leadership Development," paper presented at the Air Force Leadership—Changing Culture? Conference, RAF Museum, London, July 18–19, 2007 (University of Exeter), accessed February 1, 2023, https://business-school.exeter.ac.uk/documents/discussion_papers/cls/372.pdf.

## Chapter 17 Communicating with Confidence

1. "Jerry Seinfeld Quotes," Goodreads, accessed February 1, 2023, https://www.goodreads.com/quotes/162599-according-to-most-studies-people-s-number-one-fear-is-public.

## Chapter 18 Focusing on a Greater Purpose

1. "All Work, No Play Makes Us Unhappy Americans," *The Morning Call*, updated October 4, 2021, https://www.mcall.com/1996/12/01/all-work-no-play-makes-us-unhappy-americans/.

2. John Ortberg, *The Life You've Always Wanted: Spiritual Disciplines for Ordinary People* (Grand Rapids: Zondervan, 1997), 79.

3. Ortberg, *Life You've Always Wanted*, 81.

4. Covey, *7 Habits of Highly Effective People*, 112.

5. As quoted in James Stuart Bell and Jeanette Gardner Littleton, *Living the Serenity Prayer: True Stories of Acceptance, Courage, and Wisdom* (Avon, MA: Adams Media, 2007), 3.

**Dr. Mike Bechtle** (EdD, Arizona State University) is the author of nine books, including *People Can't Drive You Crazy If You Don't Give Them the Keys*, *Dealing with the Elephant in the Room*, and *It's Better to Bite Your Tongue Than Eat Your Words*. His articles have appeared in publications such as *Writer's Digest*, *Focus on the Family*, and *Entrepreneur*. A frequent speaker, Bechtle lives in California. Learn more at www.MikeBechtle.com.